Toward a Global Autonomous University

The Edu-factory Collective

Toward a Global Autonomous University

The Edu-factory Collective

AUTONOMEDIA

NEW YORK

Autonomedia thanks Anna Curcio, Brett Neilson, Anja Kanngieser, Rico Cleffi and Alexis Bhagat
for copyediting and proofreading, Lynette Johnston for design, and Silvia Federici for translation.

NYSCA
New York State Council on the Arts

This publication is made possible in part with public funds
from the New York State Council on the Arts, a state agency.

Autonomedia
POB 568 Williamsburgh Station
Brooklyn, NY 11211-0568 USA

info@autonomedia.org
www.autonomedia.org

Printed in the United States of America

Contents

Part III
Cognitive Labor: Conflicts and Translations

Part IV
The Production of the Common and the Global Autonomous University

Appendices

Toward a Global Autonomous University

The Edu-factory Collective

Introduction:
All Power to Self-Education!

The Edu-factory Collective

O. What was once the factory is now the university. We started off with this apparently straightforward affirmation, not in order to assume it but to question it; to open it, radically rethinking it, towards theoretical and political research. The Edu-factory project took off from here, as an assemblage of various things. It is a transnational mailing list centered around university transformations, knowledge production and forms of conflict (http://listcultures.org/mailman/listinfo/ Edu-factory_listcultures.org), in which nearly 500 activists, students and researchers the world over have taken part from the beginning. With the vanishing of state borders, global space is definitively affirmed as a space of research and political action. In this book we report on one part of our debate: the complete contributions are available on the project website (www.Edu-factory.org). Our experience over the last few years has taught us to mistrust the faith often put in the supposedly spontaneous and horizontal mechanisms that the network purportedly holds. We've learned that the network is, on the contrary, a hierarchical structure and that horizontality is continually at stake in power relationships. We've learned to flee from every technology that doesn't help us see how work is becoming more knowledge-oriented, as social relations and even the experiences of political struggle are becoming more immaterial. We've learned that the network needs to be organized or, better yet, we need to organize ourselves within the network. Grasping the radical innovation of the network-form means, therefore, approaching it as a battleground that is continually traversed by power differentials and lines of antagonistic force, from the production of the common to capitalist attempts to capture it. It is then necessary to defeat all "weak thought" of the network, which has catastrophically obscured the possibilities of surmounting representation and the political-party-form, with the villainous liquidation of the Gordian knots of organization and rupture. It is only from here that it is possible to begin the construction of those new forms of autonomous institutionality that Ned Rossiter calls organized networks.

From this perspective, Edu-factory is not only an experimentation with a new way of conducting discussions but also with a new way of organizing networks. On the one hand, the debate is temporally circumscribed and thematically identified: the two rounds of discussion — the first centered on conflicts in knowledge production, the second on processes of hierarchization in the educational marketplace and on the constitution of autonomous institutions — lasted three months each. Afterwards, the list closed to be reopened in the next cycle. This was, in other words, an attempt to pass from an extensive level to an intensive dimension of network organization. On the other hand, the list debate was scheduled around a calendar of previously planned interventions that allowed the richness of the discussion to be structured within a process of shared and focused cooperation.

Edu-factory is, above all, a partisan standpoint on the crisis of the university, which is clearly analyzed by various contributions. Already in the 1990s, Bill Readings wrote *The University in Ruins.*[1] The state university is in ruins, the mass university is in ruins, and the university as a privileged place of national culture — just like the concept of national culture itself — is in ruins. We're not suffering from nostalgia. Quite the contrary, we vindicate the university's destruction. In fact, the crisis of the university was determined by social movements in the first place. This is what makes us not merely immune to tears for the past but enemies of such a nostalgic disposition. University corporatization and the rise of a global university, to use the pregnant category proposed by Andrew Ross, are not unilateral imposition, or development, completely contained by capitalist rationality. Rather they are the result — absolutely temporary and thus reversible — of a formidable cycle of struggles. The problem is to transform the field of tension delineated by the processes analyzed in this book into specific forms of resistance and the organization of escape routes. There is no other way for us to conceive theory other than as a theoretical practice, which is partisan and subversive. This is Edu-factory's starting point and objective, its style and its method.

1. Let us return now to our initial affirmation. Might it be better to reformulate it in these terms: what was once the factory is now the university? But be careful: the university doesn't function at all like a factory. Every linear continuity risks not only being a comfortable hiding place in the categories that we were once accustomed to, but also obscuring the possibility of comprehension, and thus action, within social and productive changes. The category of knowledge factory used by Stanley Aronowitz[2] seems to us at once

allusively correct and analytically insufficient. Allusively correct because it grasps the way in which the university is becoming immediately productive, its centrality to contemporary capitalism, including its particular organizational characteristics as well as control and discipline of living labor. The reform of the Italian education system, started by Berlinguer and Zecchino, gives us a clear example — just think about the frenetic modularization of courses and the staggering acceleration of the times and rhythms of study. It is no coincidence that these were among the principal targets of the students' and precarious workers' struggles in autumn 2005.

The category of the knowledge factory, however, is analytically insufficient, since it underestimates the specific differences between the "Fordist factory" and the contemporary university. Taylorism, in fact, is something that is historically specific; it is the scientific organization of work through the temporal measurement of single tasks, execution speed and serialization. If knowledge production is not measurable, except artificially, it is evident that Taylorist production methods (through chronometers, predictability and repetition of gestures, or virtual assembly lines) are unable to organize it. The ways in which labor power is produced have changed. It is at this level and in this gap that analyses of, and possibilities for, transformation can be located.

Our initial question, if anything, indicates the urgency of a political problem: is it possible to organize within the university *as if* it were a factory? Better yet: how should we situate the political knot implied in the evocative comparison between university and factory, beginning from the incommensurable difference of their concrete functioning and their respective spatial-temporal coordinates? In other words, how can the problem of organization after the exhaustion of its traditional forms, the union and the political party, be rethought? Above all, how can it be rethought within the new composition of living labor, which no longer has an "outside"? A few lines of political research — still partially fragmentary but already quite concrete — have emerged.

If we could summarize the different global experiences that interacted in Edu-factory under a common name, it might be "self education." From the "Rete per l'autoformazione" in Rome to "Vidya Ashram" in Varanasi, from the "Universidad Experimental" in Rosario to the "Experimental College" in the United States, self-education is neither a weak niche positioned at the margins of the education system nor an entrenchment in impotent ideas and cultures gutted of resistance and subversive possibility. On the contrary, it emerged as a form of struggle for cognitive workers in contemporary capitalism. It involves, at the same time, conflict over knowledge production and the construction of the common, the struggles of precarious workers, and the organization of autonomous institutions.

Edu-factory, therefore, is a space where struggles connect, a space of resistance and organizational experiments. This is what, for example, Eileen Schell writes about concerning precarious workers' struggles in the United States: here e-learning — an instrument for the virtualization (understood here not as the power of the possible but, on the contrary, as its negation) — is turned into practices of struggle and cooperation, in a sort of open-source unionism. We shouldn't be fooled by the description of unions in universities, even though it highlights a different interpretive register with respect to the analysis of the end of the workers' movement being conducted on the other side of the Atlantic. The relation between precarious workers and unions is upside-down in a certain sense, as the important graduate student mobilization of New York University (NYU) has shown.[3] This struggle took shape as a conflict over the nature of cognitive work. While the administration refused to recognize the right of graduate students to organize a union — arguing that they are apprentices and therefore not workers — the students maintained that they are workers not only due to the fact that they sustain a large part of the teaching load, but also because they are producers of knowledge, research, and education. In these mobilizations, self-organized precarious workers affiliated themselves with the union (the United Auto Workers, in this case) that, among the range of unions, offered the most resources in economic, organizational and communicative terms. But they were prepared to change unions at any given moment; it is hardly surprising that precarious workers have no sympathy for calls for a return to a past that was sent into crisis by the conduct and movements of living labor in the first place. The question, rather, is how to link flexibility and autonomy. In this sense, the relationship with the union is disenchanted, flexible and cynical. The union should be understood as fully contained within the crisis of representation, where its structures survive, even parasitically, beyond their political function.

2. From this space where struggles are connected, the centrality of *knowledge* clearly emerges. The contributions to the Edu-factory discussion definitively take leave from the cult of knowledge, historically rooted in the left, as a sacred and intangible fetish. Not only is knowledge a peculiar kind of commodity, but it is also an instrument of hierarchization and segmentation. Nevertheless, in the moment in which it becomes a resource and a productive instrument central for contemporary capitalism, knowledge structurally exceeds the measuring units of classical political economy. It is best to clarify to avoid all misunderstandings: the excess of *living knowledge* does not coincide deterministically with its liberation.[4] We can take the case of the network and of the utopian ideas that have traversed it since its birth. The keywords — sharing, so-called horizontality, centrality of non-proprietary strategies, open source, the

excess of cooperation with respect to the market — have become the daily bread of the Prince's advisors' realism. Starting from these characteristics, which describe forms of life and work in web 2.0, the liberal legal scholar Yochai Benkler formulates his hypothesis of a "horizontal production based on common goods."[5] It is a kind of capitalism without property, where intellectual property is no longer merely the forced imposition of an artificial measure onto an immeasurable knowledge production, but an economic organization that risks blocking those very same innovative processes. In order to chase and capture living knowledge's movements, then, capital is continually compelled to modify the forms of valorization and accumulation, possibly even up to the point of putting property itself, a pilaster of modern history, into question.

In short, far from belonging to a progressive state of capitalist evolution, knowledge production is a battleground — and there is no liberation without rupture. The practices of appropriation and autonomy on one side, and the processes of capture and subsumption on the other, constitute the level of tension immanent to social cooperation. It is starting from here, from the attempt to define the analysis of the transition process that, in positive terms, was identified as the passage from "Fordism" to "postFordism" between the '80s and '90s, that Carlo Vercellone proposes the category of cognitive capitalism (the more problematic aspects of which Silvia Federici and George Caffentzis discuss). The term capitalism indicates the permanence of the capitalist system, despite its profound changes, while the attribution of "cognitive" identifies the new nature of work, the sources of valorization and the structure of property. Without going any further into a discussion developed in the various contributions here, we'd like to allow ourselves one curious annotation. On the Edu-factory list, the harshest criticisms of the concept of cognitive capitalism, which was accused of underpinning a Eurocentric analysis of the transformations to production and labor, came from Europe and North America. However, in contributions from the places in the name of which such criticisms were formulated (for example India, China, Taiwan or Argentina) a particularly rich and open dialogue developed, based on the sharing of various analytic presumptions and closer examination of a few specific points. Beyond every polemic regarding the risk of speaking in stead of others, which is to say claiming the function of representation on which postcolonial criticism has expressed words that we take as definitive, we're interested rather in underlining the fracturing of the classical image of the international division of labor. This is illustrated by the contribution of Sandro Mezzadra and Brett Neilson, which indicates the concept of the multiplication of labor as a new area of theoretical research. It is just as important to underline how Vercellone tests the concept of cognitive capitalism in the analysis of the radical, extraordinary, and victorious student struggles against the CPE (the labor laws regarding first jobs) in France during the spring of 2006. As in other experiences of conflict that in have been examined in the Edu-factory project, for example the formidable mobilizations in Greece, and the revolts in France, where the forms of *déclassement* were among the central objectives. Outside every linear image of the intellectualization of labor, these struggles allow us to read the materiality of the processes of knowledge production through social relations. Here the congnitivization of labor signifies the cognitivization of measure and exploitation, the cognitivization of class hierarchy, salary regulation and the division of labor, beyond the already surpassed dialectic between center and periphery, between first and third world. In other words, these processes permit us to situate the new field of conflict on a terrain where the processes of capitalist subsumption and valorization, far from disappearing, are compelled to recompose the forms of command over the autonomy of living knowledge, after having been forced to definitively renounce their capacity to organize them.

3. "Thus does the beginner, who has acquired a new language, keep on translating it back to his own mother tongue; only then has he grasped the spirit of the new language and is able freely to express himself therewith when he moves in it without recollections of old, and has forgotten in its use his own hereditary tongue": what Marx wrote in *The Eighteenth Brumaire of Louis Napoleon* retains its validity today. Edu-factory was in fact a laboratory for the elaboration of a common lexis that is starting to take shape in various struggles and theoretical practices on a transnational level. However, based on the relation between singularity and unity in multiplicity, common does not mean universal, a category at the center of the criticisms of Aihwa Ong. To put it clearly: common, therefore not universal. If we assume the constitutive heterogeneity of the composition of living labor on a global level, or what has been defined as multitudes, as the material base of our activities, the classical formula of communication of social struggles and their languages doesn't work anymore. It is here that, not wanting to abandon the contemplation of the proliferation of differences in a multicultural perspective and therefore assuming the impossibility of a comprehensive transformation of social relations, the concept of translation illustrated by Naoki Sakai and Jon Solomon offers a materialistic theory of the new composition of living labor and the production of the common. Various contributions — from Amit Basole to Nirmal Puwar and Sanjay Sharma — insist on the criticism of disciplinary and Eurocentric codes through which the Anglophone model of the university has spread. Even though sometimes, it should be added, the criticism of Eurocentrism risks becoming a weak cliché, nostalgic of local traditions and mythological roots or, even worse, a rhetorical arm of the emergent postcolonial elite. We could then say that the global university is constituted through a continual monolingual translation of multiplicity into the abstract homogeneity of the universal: "in

this mode of communication, the enunciating subject addresses the receiver of the discourse assuming the stability and the homogeneity as much of his/her own language as that of s/he who hears is; even when the two languages are different, the 'locutor' speaks as if the interlocutor belonged to his/her same linguistic community, assigning the job of rendering transparent the communication to the translation and so reproducing the supremacy — true sovereignty — of his/her language."[6] For example, in Italy the feudal governance still in effect in universities is not in contradiction with the corporatizing processes but rather guides it in the particular form of translation. Thus the conservative resistance to the "university mandarins," the defense of the sacredness of knowledge and the nostalgia for ivory towers are not only useless, but also entirely reactionary. It is rather a question of situating the movement on a line of a transforming resistance that assumes the ambivalence of the new context as a terrain of struggle. In fact, the interruption of the capitalist tradition does not mean a return to the national university, it rather poses the problem of heterolingual translation, or the construction of the common starting from the multiplicity of forms of resistance and from movements of living knowledge, assuming "the foreignness of all of the parts involved as the starting point independent from their 'lingua natia.' Here, translation is the language of a subject in transit."[7] Singularities are not recomposed in a mythical original essence or in a new sovereign machine, but find the resource and the stakes of their own forms of language and relations in the common. Heterolingual translation moves from an autonomous spatial-temporal dimension that intersects the global capitalist space but never coincides with it — it interrupts it, flips it, and continually exceeds it.

Using the 20th-century labor movement's categories, we could say that heterolingual translation is internal to class composition, which is to say the relation between technical and political composition. Since these categories — incarnated in a historically determined subject, the working class, and based on the spatial-temporal linearity of the factory — can no longer be proposed in the same form in which the labor movement forged them, they consequently must be rethought from the beginning. In the relation between singularity and the production of the common, in the multitudes, the articulation of differences can acquire a disjunctive sense, in the measure in which singularities are lead to the identity of a presumed belonging (ethnic, sexual, communitarian, or social group). This is the technical composition that sustains the processes of differential inclusion. Here conflict doesn't go beyond politically recognizing one's own position in the capitalist hierarchy. We have confronted this limit in different mobilizations of precarious workers, for example in that of the researchers against the Moratti Reform in Italy. Their strength dissolved when they explicitly or implicitly identified themselves in specific categories (knowledge workers, the creative class, the "most intelligent part of the country"), which are not at all descriptive, but rather prescriptive. They are, in other terms, decomposition factors and rearticulations of common instances in key sectors; a sort of new identity of a middle class after its end, or the mediation and conservation of a social equilibrium of exploitative relations. Besides, the concept of cognitive labor — that, as Ross suggests, finds a paradigmatic anticipation in the forms of academic work — radically differentiates itself from the above indicated categories in the measure in which it is to be understood as the grid through which the entire composition of living labor and its transformations is to be read. We can accordingly redefine political composition as a process of dis-identification,[8] of disarticulation of the technical composition and of a new composition on a "line of force" that finds its definition in the production of the common. Let's call this line of force "class." Against any possible sociological and economic interpretation, class is at stake in of a process of struggle, it is not its objective precondition. Between technical composition and political composition, between capitalist hierarchy and the differential potential of conflicts, there is a power relation, not a homology and symmetry. With these new spatial-temporal coordinates, in the student and precarious worker struggles from China to the United States, from Greece to Italy, from South Africa to France, through the possible processes of heterolingual translation and construction of common lexis and practices, our initial hypothesis about the university and the factory takes on a new hue. How can we transform the university into a political space for struggle and exodus, for the political composition of differences in a space-time of class, just as the factory was for the working class? Beyond, or rather against any naïve continuum, this is the political *raison d'être* of Edu-factory.

4. The experiences of conflict that have been brought into relation through Edu-factory are situated within, or better said, inside and against the tranformations of the university. The contributions collected here provide an important grid to read the trends that are common on a transnational level and that find their own adaptations — in fact their own translations — in different contexts. These are the new spatial coordinates, which Wang Hui, Ranabir Samaddar, Franco Barchiesi and Stanley Aronowitz give as an outline in their respective contributions to Edu-factory, some available in this book and others available on the website as video interviews. According to these coordinates, the nation-state ceases to be the measure of analysis of the current changes, as the attempt to construct a European space of higher education, also known as the Bologna Process, demonstrates. In this framework, Toby Miller and Xiang Biao accurately profile the hierarchization process through which the education market is constituted, inside which the university — having re-

signed every pretext of exclusivity over the forms of production and transmission of knowledge — is located. The lively discussion on the list also permitted us to qualify the corporatization process of the education system in terms both more precise and qualitatively different from the currently diffused rhetoric. It is not simply a matter of public disinvestment and the growing private investment in the higher education sector: rather, it is the very dialectic between public and private that is breaking down. In fact, as Marc Bousquet demonstrates, it is the university that is becoming corporate and functioning according to the parameters of the corporate world. At the same time, as Ross persipicuously suggests, the "knowledge business" is modeling itself by importing conditions, mentalities, and habits from academic labor. Starting in the 80s, the theory of New Public Management, defined as a movement of thought and philosophy of public sector reform, was charged with managing the introduction of instruments and a logic of private organization into the university. Any recourse to the state against business has no sense today, if it ever did. The state, just like the "mandarin" government in universities, is in fact the guarantor of corporatization, going so far as to cease distinguishing between itself and private organizations. The alterations in the university should therefore be framed within the crisis of welfare. The conflictual genealogy of this crisis — which includes the radical criticism of the devices for disciplining the labor force and their universalistic and neutralizing systems, which chronologically and politically precede neoliberal reconstruction — illustrates the level of the current struggle. A struggle that, again, sheds no tears for the past.

In global space, as Mezzadra and Neilson suggest, borders decompose, recompose and multiply all at the same time. This is also true of the relation between the university and the metropolis. Once again, the example of NYU — a global brand of higher education — assumes paradigmatic traits in this regard. In fact, in New York two principle agents of gentrification, or studentification as it has been significantly defined, are universities: Colombia University in West Harlem and NYU on the Lower East Side. But if in the first case the borders of the campus are expanded to include a new zone, in the case of NYU the borders seem to dissolve in a mimetic relationship with the metropolitan fabric. So much so, that for NYU President John Sexton and the university's administration, which comes entirely from the corporate world, the challenge is rethinking the metropolitan development of New York starting from the university, guiding the passage from the FIRE economy, based on finance, insurance and real estate, to a ICE economy, or the valorizing of intellectual, cultural and education resources. The borders, therefore, that become porous till the point of nearly dissolving themselves into the relationship between the corporate university and the metropolis, are continually retraced in order to subsume the knowledge production diffused in social cooperation. It isn't by chance that the Lower East Side was a historic zone for sprouting movements and independent cultures, before becoming a development of Silicon Ally, the high-tech end of the Big Apple, during the '90s and now a potential motor for the ICE economy. Gentrification and studentification are open processes that transform the social composition and open new fields of conflict. In these processes we see the entire composition of labor commanded by revenue spread, according to the form of contemporary capitalist subsumption: from precarious labor in the universities to janitors and third-sector service workers. All this contributes to render metropolitan spaces valuable in so far as they are relational and cooperative fabrics, with the decisive role being played by finance and investments in urban transformations. Here, too, there is little to defend or conserve: what is left over is usually residual and sometimes even an obstacle to the possibility of liberation. Reconfiguring studentification in an antagonistic sense, attacking its dynamic on a deep level means, at the very least, rethinking the metropolis; constructing the university-metropolis starting with institutions of the common.

Since there is nothing external to the relationship between the university and the metropolis anymore, the mechanisms of selection and segmentation change too. They are no longer based on exclusion, or the rigid confine between who is "in" and who is "out," but on processes of differential inclusion. In other words, in the framework of a permanent credit system, the level of qualification of the work force, as demonstrated by Xiang Biao starting from the case in China, doesn't depend so much on the fact that individuals have a university degree or not, but above all on which educational institution they attended and the position of this institution on the hierarchy of the educational market. To put it in synthetic terms, with reference to the Italian situation: if up until the 1960s the bottleneck of selection was quite narrow, jammed between the completion of high school and entrance to the university, it became gradually wider, pressured by social movements long before the capitalist system's need for endogenous rationalization. In fact it was '68 that shattered the bottleneck, inaugurating what would be called the mass university. Now the problem for the Italian government isn't restricting access but augmenting it, in order to keep up with European and international statistics. However, the inclusion process is accompanied by a dequalification of knowledge, most of all those kinds of knowledge that are normally recognized. What is called the highschoolization of the university means that students must climb the ladder to earn or, better yet, credit themselves with skills expendable on the job market. In this situation, the old expression "the right to education" loses meaning, to the extent in which conflict shifts to the quality of inclusion and knowledge production as new hierarchization devices.

Here are the lines of intersection between the making precarious of academic work precarious and the imposition of new cognitive measures that range from the system of intellectual property and educational credits all the way to their corresponding characteristic, debt — a question elaborated in detail by Jeffery Williams in the American context. Here a new student figure is embodied, no longer as a member of the work force in training, but as a worker Recent literature shows decisive analytical traces of this change.[9] It is within this framework that the university assumes a new role insofar as it is one of the many nodes and devices of metropolitan control, which artificially measure and regulate the value of cognitive labor power through skill stratification and intellectual qualification. This artificial measure not only lacks an objective character but also loses the capacity to accurately describe the abilities of single workers. Aihwa Ong[10] and Xiang Biao[11] (who have both actively taken part in our list discussions) have demonstrated this in particularly convincing ways, for example in the case of the Indian "technomigrants," who represent the motor of development in Silicon Valley as well as in the Australian high-tech industry. These figures are forced to drive taxis or work low wage jobs to be able to reach an income sufficient to sustain their mobility and negotiate the immigration politics in order to enter or stay in the country. The forms of differential inclusion that affect the changing figure of the citizen also pass through the imposition of borders regulated by artificial cognitive measures. The above cited texts, just like the whole experience of Edu-factory, invite us to break away from traditional points of view in reading these changes in the educational system and in cognitive labor. The same applies to biocapital — here intended in a very specific sense: the way in which social relations unfold in the processes of capital invested in biotechnologies.[12] This is not because centers and peripheries don't exist anymore in absolute but because their relation breaks up and rearticulates itself continually in the metropolis in so far as it is an immediately global space. Above all, this relation doesn't follow the traditional dividing lines of the global market anymore. Hence, if we do not look to what is happening in China or India, in Singapore or in Taiwan, we exclude ourselves from the possibility of grasping the world's becoming one and therefore our ability to transform it.

5. Edu-factory is a project situated on the frontier: between the university and the metropolis, between education and labor, between the rubble of the past and exodus, between the crisis of the university and the organization of the common. Whereas the border imposes a dividing line, the frontier is a dense space, ambivalent and traversable, a place of escape and constituent practices. There is a productive force on the frontier that can be explored and appropriated in antagonistic ways. Here, there is a reconfiguration of the spatial and

temporal coordinates in which the crisis of the university can be questioned and fought. We could say that the relation between cognitive labor and subsumption processes are configured primarily as a conflict over time, which not by chance has been a central focus of the student and precarious worker struggles around the world. The creation of artificial units of cognitive measure that try to maintain the vigilance of the law of value where it has long ceased to be valid configures itself — to cite Walter Benjamin — as the imposition of the empty and homogeneous time of capital on the full and heterogeneous times of living knowledge. Or, in Marx's terms, as a continual reduction — a monolingual translation — of living knowledge's production times to time units of abstract labor. The concept of the common is materially incarnated as beginning with the temporality of living knowledge, a concept that we can find in the contributions of Stefano Harney and Fred Moten, of Jason Read and James Arvanitakis. The common is, from a class point of view, the escape route from the crisis of the public/private dialectic to which we previously alluded. It would be useful to clear up one point, which constitutes a subject of divergent readings on the question of the commons in the Italian and transnational debate. When we speak about the common we are not referring to a good to be defended or protected, but to the affirmation of social cooperation's autonomy and self-organization. The common, far from existing in nature, is therefore produced: it is always at stake in constituent processes, capable of destroying relations of exploitation and liberating the power of living labor.

The common isn't the umpteenth repositioning of a new dawn, or a weak preconfiguration of utopian hope. The common is that which lives in the present, a full virtuality, intended this time as the potentiality of the actual. The paths of self-education confronted in Edu-factory are not marginal spaces but, to use the categories of Chandra Talpade Mohanty, new spatialtemporal coordinates for the production of oppositional knowledges and the organization of living knowledge's autonomy. They are expressions from the point of view and practices of minority agents. The debate about autonomous institutions begins with the abandoning of majority thought, the empty temporality of the abstract subject, and the export of universal models. This theme (which was discussed not only on the Edu-factory list but also in other important political formats, for example the European web journal "Transform" (http://transform.eipcp.net) and Uninomade, which furnishes Toni Negri and Judith Revel's contribution that closes the present volume), is both an innovative project of theoretic research and a political program. How do we reply to the question: why pose the theme of autonomous institutions with such urgency? We could answer as follows: because the exodus is already upon us. We've experimented with it in the political and social expressions of what we call multitude. And nevertheless we would have to add: exodus does not naturally coincide with autonomy. Exodus must conquer autonomous organization by organizing its own institutions.

There are a few historically important examples. One is the case of Black Studies in the United States. Far from belonging to the progressive evolution of academic disciplines or in the national integration processes, Black Studies began with the barricades of the 1968 Third World Strike in San Francisco, the affirmations of the Black Power movement, and the rifles on the shoulders of black students at Cornell University. Just as, Mohanty suggests, postcolonial studies becomes a soothing postmodern phenomenon if its genealogy is not traced back to anticolonial struggles, those who would still think that knowledge production belongs to the irenic field of cultural and scientific objectivity are finally forced to reconsider. In a recent book dedicated to this extraordinary history, Noliwe Rooks[13] clarifies how the passage of the Black movement from the lexis of rights to the exercise of power has nothing to do with the third internationalist idea of taking control of the state or with the symmetrically opposite positions of John Holloway. Rather, it involved the rupture of democratic integration and the constitution of separate institutions, autonomously controlled and self-managed by the Black community. It was the attempt to change the word exercising power relations *hic et nunc* in complete independence from the state. The response to the institutional organization of exodus and separation is concretized in a lethal articulation of brutal repression and differential inclusion, the sum of which is represented by the Ford Foundation's strategies. Rooks briefly lingers on the selective financing of Black communities and Black Studies to favor the leaders of the groups that sustained the cause of racial integration and attempted to marginalize radical militants. University governance here is a response to struggles and autonomous organization: inclusion becomes a device of control and, where this is not possible, it is always ready to exercise violence.

Analogously, today the forms of university governance cannot allow themselves to uproot self-education. To the contrary, self-education constitutes a vital sap for the survival of the institutional ruins, snatched up and rendered valuable in the form of revenue. Governance is the trap, hasty and flexible, of the common. Instead of countering us frontally, the enemy follows us: the origin of this asymmetrical conflict is the ungovernability and infidelity of living labor. That means, on one hand, that governance is permanently faced with its own crisis, which is genealogically determined by the autonomy of living knowledge and the impossibility of vertical government. On the other hand, we must immediately reject any weak interpretation of the theme of autonomous institutions, according to which the institution is a self-governed structure that lives between the folds of capitalism, without excessively bothering it. In the worst cases, this can even become individual entrepreneurship. So, the institutionalization of self-education doesn't mean being recognized as one actor among many within the education market, but the capacity to organize living knowledge's autonomy and resistance. This means determining command and collective direction within social cooperation, as well as producing common norms that destructure the existing university. It involves the institution of a new temporal relation — nonlinear and anti-dialectic, full and heterogeneous — between crisis and decision, between constituent processes and concrete political forms, between the event and organizational sedimentation, between rupture and the production of the common. These are relations that, to the extent in which they are immanent to class composition and the temporality of conflict, break with the presumption of a general will and with power's sovereign transcendence. They force an opening towards the potentiality of the actual. This is why common institutions are continually traversed by the possibility of their subversion. To paraphrase Marx, the autonomous institution is the concrete political form of common possession which is the base of individual property.

From this point of view, Edu-factory allows us to map the global geography of autonomous institutionality. The investigational method utilized by the Counter Cartographies collective reveals itself not only as a learning tool, but also as a constitutive process. In self-educational experiences, knowledge — whose power devices are revealed by detailed analyses of Sunil Sahasrabudhey and Randy Martin — is disarticulated and composed along new lines. Knowledge production in this context is therefore the refusal of transmitted knowledge from the rubble of the university. Better yet: refusal is the full affirmation of the autonomous subject. It is non-cooperative production, to use Vidya Ashram's words, or productive cooperation against and beyond capital. In this direction, the European prospective — used in Italy as an instrument of legitimation for the center-left's university reform and then abruptly abandoned to national regurgitations in the face of an impasse — should be taken up once again, beginning from the institutionality of the common. It is on this base that the project for a Global Autonomous University, which is elaborated in Vidya Ashram's contribution in this book, was born. This project does not seek for recognition in the education market, but rather to expose its mechanisms. Here the descriptive plane meets the project's prescriptivism, and theoretical research opens towards a political program. Here the blueprints are drawn for a sort of Edu-factory 2.0, no longer merely a space of discussion and connections, but of common organization.

6. We started with the crisis of the university, and this is also where we will conclude — or better yet, with the intimate liaison between this crisis and the global economic crisis. It is precisely this double crisis that students and precarious workers refuse to pay for. We Won't Pay for Your Crisis is, not coin-

cidentally, the slogan that characterized the Italian movement, known as the Anomalous Wave (www.uniriot.org) in the final months of 2008. In any case, the "communism of capital" recently evoked by *The Economist* is nothing other than the continuing subsumption of living knowledge and its production of the common in the accumulative regimes of the productive metropolis and its ganglion nerve centers, such as the corporate university. In the "communism of capital," crisis is no longer a cyclical fact but a permanent element.

The conflicts that arise with the interlacing of these two processes are at the center of this book. As these social struggles demonstrate, the time of crisis also offers great possibility. It shouldn't be stopped, but assaulted. The slogan that accompanies the "wild demonstrations" — or those protests that are not officially organized in compliance with local laws — of students and precarious workers clearly delineates the two parts of theconflict: on one hand impeding the conservation of the existent, and on the other, the force of transformation. On one side the resignation of the university system, on the other, the autonomy of living knowledge. There is nothing in-between: representative institutions are skipped over because the movement is irrepresentable. In fact, the movement is already an institution itself, absorbing even the functions of political mediation within autonomous organization and definitively removing them from representative structures. The task now is to render the "self-reform of the university" — that these social movements are accomplishing through struggles and practicing with self-education — a comprehensive project.

This also allows us to rethink the theme of freedom in materialistic terms — a theme evoked just as much by the forms of labor and the transformations of the university as it is systematically restricted by precariousness, educational programs and differential modes of higher education financing. This is an ample research area that we'd simply like to flag as urgent. If freedom is understood in the classical sense, as freedom of opinion, it is not negated but rather required by the new regime of accumulation. It is an indispensable productive resource and source of identity for the creative and the knowledge worker. Thus, freedom becomes radical criticism of exploitation only if it is incarnated in the autonomous potency of living knowledge instead of within simple power relations. The freedom of the common is partisan.

We've already mentioned it, and with this we'll conclude: a few years ago "changing the world without taking power" became diffused rhetoric and an inflated refrain. It created more problems than it resolved. Above and beyond an obvious contestation that was already true for the class composition that destructured Fordism, it misconstrued the concept of power, flattening it onto the state. The exercise of power, immanent to power relations and class composition, is rather a condition of possibility for common organization and the rupturing of the political unity of the state. In this movement, exodus becomes living knowledge's autonomy. We need to take a step back to avoid having to restart from the beginning. Therefore, after having recognized the irreducibility of living knowledge's excess and the diffuseness of the network form, we now have to combine spatial extensionality with temporal intensity, the accumulation of force with the verticality of rupture. Let us end with a phrase that despite its being a bit antiquated perfectly summarizes the situation: autonomous institutions of the common are the terrain on which to rethink the actuality of revolution after its classical forms have been definitively exhausted. The university is, for us, one of the possible spaces for experimenting with this revolution.

Notes

[1] Readings, B. (1996), *The University in Ruins,* Harvard University Press, Cambridge – London.

[2] Aronowitz, S. (2000), *The Knowledge Factory. Dismantling the Corporate University and Creating True Higher Learning,* Beacon Press, Boston, Mass.

[3] Krause, M., Nolan, M., Palm, M., Ross, A. (2008), *The University Against Itself. The NYU Strike and the Future of the Academic Workplace,* Temple University Press, Philadelphia.

[4] Cfr. Alquati, R. (1976), "L'università e la formazione: l'incorporazione del sapere sociale nel lavoro vivo," in *Aut Aut,* Firenze, n. 154.

[5] Benkler, Y. (2007), *La ricchezza della rete. La produzione sociale trasforma il mercato e aumenta le libertà,* Università Bocconi Editore, Milano.

[6] Mezzadra, S. (2008), *La condizione postcoloniale. Storia e politica nel presente globale,* Ombre Corte, Verona, p. 108.

[7] Ivi, pp. 125–126.

[8] Cfr. Rancière, J. (2007), *Il disaccordo,* Meltemi, Roma.

[9] Cfr. Bousquet, M. (2008), *How the University Works. Higher Education and the Low-Wage Nation,* New York University Press, New York – London.

[10] Ong, A. (2006), *Neoliberalism as Exception. Mutations in Citizenship and Sovereignty,* Duke University Press, Durham, NC – London.

[11] Xiang, B. (2007), *Global "Body Shopping": An Indian Labor System in the Information Technology Industry,* Princeton University Press, Princeton.

[12] Rajan, K. S. (2006), *Biocapital. The Constitution of Postgenomic Life,* Duke University Press, Durham, NC – London.

[13] Rooks, N. M. (2006), *White Money – Black Power. The Surprising History of African American Studies and the Crisis of Race in Higher Education,* Beacon Press, Boston.

PART I

The Production of Knowledge in the Global University

The Rise of the Global University

Andrew Ross

As universities are increasingly exposed to the rough justice of the market, we have seen how their institutional life is distinguished more by the rate of change than by the observance of custom and tradition. Few examples illustrate this better than the rush, in recent years, to establish overseas programs and branch campuses. Since 9/11, the pace of offshoring has surged and is being pursued across the entire spectrum of institutions that populate the higher education landscape — from the ballooning for-profit sectors and online diploma mills to land grant universities to the most elite, ivied colleges. No single organization has attained the operational status of a global university, after the model of the global corporation, but it is only a matter of time before we see the current infants of that species take their first, unaided steps. The WTO has been pushing trade services liberalization for several years, of which higher educational services are a highly prized component, with an estimated global market of between $40 and $50 billion (not much less than the market for financial services). Opponents of liberalization argue that higher education cannot and should not be subject to the kind of free trade agreements that have been applied to commercial goods and other services in the global economy. After all, WTO agreements would guarantee foreign service providers the same rights that apply to domestic providers within any national education system while compromising the sovereignty of national regulatory efforts. Yet the evidence shows that, just as corporations did not wait for the WTO to conclude its ministerial rounds before moving their operations offshore, the lack of any international accords has not stopped universities in the leading Anglophone countries from establishing their names and services in a broad range of overseas locations. The formidable projected growth in student enrollment internationally, combined with the expansion of technological capacity and the consolidation of English as a lingua franca have resulted in a bonanza-style environment for investors in offshore education.

As with any other commodity, good or service that is allowed to roam across borders, there has also been much hand-wringing about the potential lack of quality assurance. Critics argue that the caliber of education will surely be jeopardized if the global market for it is deregulated. Much less has been said in this debate about the impact on the working conditions of academics or on the ethical profile and aspirational identity of institutions. How will globalization affect the security and integrity of livelihoods that are closely tied to liberal educational ideals like meritocratic access, face-to-face learning, and the disinterested pursuit of knowledge? Will these ideals (and the job base built around them) wither away entirely in the entrepreneurial race to compete for a global market share, or will they survive only in one corner of the market — as the elite preserve of those who are able to pay top dollar for such hand-crafted attention?

Lessons from the China Field

While researching my last book, *Fast Boat to China,* I did a year of field work in several Yangtze River Delta cities. Once I had wangled a membership in the American Chamber of Commerce in Shanghai, I spent a lot of time attending meetings and functions of that organization. It proved to be a wonderful research site to gather data about the offshore business climate, since almost every speculator on the planet eventually shows up there, expecting to make a fast buck. One of the best vantage points to watch this seedy spectacle was at the Chamber's social mixers, usually hosted in one of the city's toniest nightspots, and crafted to ensure a frenzy of networking, promotional pitching, and deal-making. Though I was a regular attender at these mixers, I was invariably taken for a musician (no doubt, because of my physical appearance), who was circulating in the crowd before being called upon to perform. How to dispel this perception? As an ethnographer who wanted to clarify his real identity, my opening gambit in conversation was often something along the lines of "Hello, I'm not here to make money, I just study people who do," but, despite all such efforts, my interlocutors found it almost impossible to resist pitching their business models to me, just in case I might want to invest.

Indeed, wherever I went on my research trips in China, I was treated as a potential investor (at least after it was established that I was not in fact a musician). It took me a little while to realize that this treatment had less to do with the fact that I was a foreigner than that I was an academic. My business card, after all, revealed my connection with NYU, and NYU is a huge brand in

China's private sector, much revered on account of its Stern business school which contributes in no small measure to that country's "MBA fever." So I was automatically accorded some attention, and must confess that, since the Stern name was opening doors for my research needs, I did not go out of my way to decline the opportunities generated by this misplaced association.

In addition, however, and more significantly, as I discovered after two or three mixers, many of the people most likely to be propping up the bar at these Chamber of Commerce events were representatives of American universities. Some were there for purely social reasons — to make friends and romantic connections — but all of them were ready to pitch their wares as and when the opportunity arose. Desperate for management expertise, the Chinese government, as early as 1991, began to authorize foreign universities to offer MBA and EMBA programs. Shanghai, earmarked for top-drawer development as Asia's new financial capital, became the epicenter for the joint-partnered or wholly transplanted degree programs offered by such universities, with Washington University and USC leading the pack. In the last few years, other kinds of academic programs have followed suit, especially in industrial sectors crucial to China's economic growth: engineering, applied science, and tourism management. Skyrocketing tuition fees, long absences from home, the Asian financial crisis of the late 1990s, and, since 9/11, visa restrictions, have sharply reduced the flow of Asian students to the U.S. More and more of our revenue-hungry institutions have gone offshore to service these students in their home countries.

After talking to these reps at the bar, and watching them interact with the corporate investors in the room, I came to realize that, as a representative of an American university, I was not at all out of place in this environment. My institutional employer and its "brand" were perfectly at home in this watering-hole for profit-chasing, cost-cutting investors chasing a lucrative offshore opportunity. It's one thing to joke in the faculty lounge about our universities going off in pursuit of emerging global markets, and yet another to be handed a business card in such an emerging market by corporate reps who want to do business with you and who assume exactly the same of you. My personal experience in China helped me understand how easy it is, in practice, for our academic culture to meld with the normalizing assumptions and customs of corporate business culture.

Certainly, it was easy to see how the academic reps might be influenced by the maverick mentality of these investors. But it is more important to grasp why the investors might feel they have something to learn, and profit materially, from the successes of American higher education in the business of overseas penetration. After all, the history of foreign involvement in China in the nineteenth century was the dual record of missionary educators and business people, the one pursuing a potential harvest of 400 million minds and souls, the other seduced by the lure of 400 million consumer converts, each community providing cover for the other's activities. Arguably, the religious educators were more successful. Many of the colleges that American missionaries established have morphed over the decades into China's top universities, and, in addition, the lure of American higher education for Chinese students has proven to be quite enduring. Such things are not lost on the keen business mind.

Given the rate at which American universities are setting up shop in China, it is no surprise that NYU opened its own program in Shanghai in September 2006, bringing its list of study abroad locations to eight: the others are in London, Paris, Madrid, Berlin, Prague, Florence, and Accra. At the time of writing, the Shanghai site is one of several locations being considered as branch campuses of NYU (the most controversial being in Abu Dhabi) registered to offer degrees to students who will not have attended the domestic U.S. campus. The decision about whether to offer a range of degrees abroad to local nationals is one which several universities had already made. It remained to be seen whether this move would be fully debated in light of the experience of these other colleges, and how such a decision would affect the character and resource-map of the institution. Open deliberation on this question would surely help address the ailing state of faculty governance at NYU. It might also pressure the administration to observe some measure of transparency in policy decision-making. But in practice, NYU, like its peers, had long ago crossed that threshold, and in the larger world of higher education, the distinction between onshore and offshore education — like that between private and public, or non-profit and for-profit — had become very blurry indeed.

The distinction matters even less when viewed from the perspective of how the export trade in educational services is defined. The WTO, for example, recognizes four categories under this heading. Mode 1 involves arms-length or cross-border supply such as distance learning. Mode 2 is consumption abroad, which is primarily covered by international students studying overseas, enrolled at institutions in the U.S. for example. Mode 3 is commercial presence, basically foreign direct investment in the form of satellite branches of institutions, and Mode 4 is movement of natural persons — such as academics teaching abroad. All the current and foreseeable growth is in Mode 1 and Mode 3, and much of this is assumed to be linked to a perceived decline in Mode 2 growth. Statisticians justify their own trade as well the core principles of free trade by showing how these patterns of ebb and flow are interconnected. In response, and as a general fiscal principle, organizations will try to balance their budgets by pushing expansion in one area to compensate for shortfalls in another. This is how global firms have learned to operate, by assessing and equalizing the relative return on their investments in various parts of the world, both in the world of real revenue and in the more speculative realm of brand-building for the future. University accounting departments have begun to juggle their budgets in a similar way. A deep revenue stream from a facility in the Middle East will be viewed as a way to subsidize unprofitable humanities programs at home (as is the case at one Midwestern institution where I inquired) just as an onshore science center capable of capturing U.S. federal grant money may be incubated to help fund an Asian venture considered crucial to brand-building in the region.

A Balance of Trade

In the interviews I conducted with faculty and administrators at NYU and elsewhere, a clear pattern of talk about this kind of fiscal juggling emerged (though no hard numbers could be accessed with which to match the rhetoric). NYU's own global programs are an eclectic mix of ventures, spread across several schools and divisions, each of which has its own fiscal boat to float. When viewed in their entirety, it is clear that the programs do not hold to any overall rule about the demarcation of onshore from offshore education, let alone any systematic educational philosophy. Though they lack a coherent profile, they show a clear pattern of exponential growth and expansion onto every continent — beginning, historically, with the Madrid and Paris study abroad programs in "Old" Europe — and into each regional market as it was declared open to foreign direct investment.

While its eight study abroad sites are primarily for NYU students to send a semester abroad, places are offered to non-NYU students as and when vacancies open up. In addition, as many as sixty summer study abroad programs are currently offered to non-NYU students in Brazil, Canada, China, Cuba, Czech Republic, England, France, Germany, Ghana, Greece, Ireland, Italy, Mexico, Netherlands, Russia, South Africa, Spain, Sweden and Switzerland. The absence, from New York, during the Fall and Spring semesters, of a quarter (and, by 2011, a half) of its students allows NYU the option of increasing enrollment, or of reducing the costly expense of providing leased dorm space in downtown Manhattan. Either option has a huge impact on revenue, and seems to be a primary motivation not only for university policy in this area, but also for other colleges to emulate NYU's successful fiscal example. By 1998, less than a decade after incoming president Jay Oliva pledged to shape a global university to match Ed Koch's global city aspirations for New York itself, NYU had outstripped all other American universities in the volume of students it sent overseas. It also enrolled the highest number of international students. Oliva was known internationally as the founder and host of the League of World Universities, whose rectors met regularly in New York to discuss how to respond to the challenge of globalization, and his successor John Sexton had made his name by pioneering a Global Law program as Dean of the NYU Law School.

In the years since then, NYU has found itself in the forefront of online efforts to offer distance learning abroad (one of which, NYU Online, was a notorious $20 million casualty of the dot.com bust, though its successor has thrived) while each of its schools has been encouraged to make global connections. The Stern business school entered into partnership with the London School of Economics and the Ecole des Hautes Etudes Commerciales to offer an EMBA on a global basis, the law school set up an LLM program in Singapore for students from the Asia region, and the Tisch School of the Arts also chose Singapore as the location for a new Master's program in film production. The scale of the university's proposed joint venture with the American University in Paris (AUP) has upped the ante. While it is not likely to involve more than a small minority of NYU students, its growth potential is tied to recruiting well beyond the 800 international students currently enrolled by the AUP.

Less conspicuously, perhaps, NYU's School of Continuing and Professional Studies (SCPS), which educates more than 50,000 adult learners annually in more than 125 fields, has become widely known for its provision of services abroad. This has even extended to graduate programs, which it has offered online since 1994, first through the Virtual College and now through NYU Online. SCPS was one of the first university institutions in the U.S. to register with the Department of Commerce's BUYUSA program, officially described as "an electronic marketplace that connects U.S. exporters with qualified agents, buyers, and partners overseas." In the words of one of the school's assistant deans, this program has helped SCPS to locate agents and partners in countries that they "never would have considered otherwise." Examples of the school's penetration in the China market include instructional seminars offered to executives in that country's publishing industry, and a program in real estate finance designed for brokers and developers active in the PRC's vast construction boom. SCPS is a hugely profitable arm of NYU, and its instruction is carried by an almost wholly adjunct workforce whose compensation in no way reflects the lucrative revenue harvested by course offerings in such nonorthodox disciplines as Philanthropy and Fundraising, Life Planning, Food and Wine, and Real Estate.

Not surprisingly, SCPS was one of the first educational institutions to receive the President's Export Award for its work in promoting U.S. educational services overseas. In the U.S. trade balance, education is the fifth largest export service, bringing in $12 billion in 2004, and arguably the one with the biggest growth potential. In New Zealand, and Australia, among the other leaders in this field of trade, education is the third and fourth largest export services. Given the intensification of the global competition for high-skill jobs, educational services are increasingly a number one commodity in fast-developing countries. The Department of Commerce will help any U.S. university to develop this trade, here or abroad, in much the same way as it helps corporations. For relatively small fees, its Commercial Service will organize booths at international education fairs, find an international partner for one of your university's ventures, help it with brand recognition in a new market, perform market research, and, through use of the premium Platinum Key Service, offer six months of expertise on setting up an overseas campus and marketing said campus in one of over 80 countries.

The Race to Deregulate

The Commerce Department's activities are fully aligned with the trade liberalization agenda of the WTO, where higher education falls under the General Agreement on Trade and Services (GATS). Dedicated, like all WTO agencies, to the principle that free trade is the best guarantee of best quality at lowest cost, GATS was formed in 1995, and higher education services were added to its jurisdiction largely as a result of pressure in 2000 from the United States representative to the WTO, backed by representatives from Australia, New Zealand, and Japan. This inclusion has been fiercely opposed by most higher education leaders in WTO member nations, most prominently by a 2001 Joint Declaration of four large academic organizations in North America and Europe (http://www.eua.be/eua/) and the 2002 Porto Alegre Declaration, signed by Iberian and Latin American associations (www.gatswatch.org/educationoutofgats/PortoAlegre.doc). The signatories of these two declarations agree that trade liberalization risks weakening governments' commitment to — and investment in — public higher education, that education is not a commodity but a basic human right, and that its reliance on public mandates should make it distinct from other services. Yet the concerted opposition of these professional bodies has made little difference to the 45 countries (EU counts as one) that had already made commitments to the education sector by January 2006. Indeed if the current round of WTO negotiations, the Doha Round, had not been logjammed by acrimonious disagreements over agricultural trade, GATS would have concluded its work some time ago, imposing severe constraints on individual government's rights to regulate education within their borders.

Such constraints are particularly debilitating to developing countries who will lose valuable domestic regulatory protection from the predatory advances of service providers from rich nations. Indeed, a new ministerial mandate at GATS allows demandeurs like the US, New Zealand, and Australia to band together to put plurilateral pressure on the poorer target countries to accept their education exports (demandeur governments are those doing the asking position under the WTO's request-offer process). Officially, GATS is supposed to exclude services "supplied in the exercise of governmental authority" — by nonprofit educational organizations — but most nations that are committed have chosen not to clarify the distinction between non-profit and for-profit. With good reason, we can expect creeping, if not galloping, liberalization in all sectors if the GATS trade regime proceeds. After all, the free trade culture of WTO is one in which public services are automatically seen as unfair government monopolies, and should be turned over to private for-profit providers whenever possible, all in the name of "full market access." From the standpoint of teaching labor, this tendency points in the direction of increasing precarity — an interim environment of job insecurity, de-professionalization and ever-eroding faculty governance in institutions stripped of their public service obligations and respect for academic freedom.

Even in the absence of any such formal trade regime, we have seen the clear impact of market liberalization at all levels of higher education; the voluntary introduction of revenue center management models where every departmental unit has to prove itself as a profit center; the centralization of power upward into managerial bureaucracies; the near-abdication of peer review assessment in research units that are in bed with industry; the casualization of the majority of the academic workforce, for whom basic professional tenets like academic freedom are little more than a mirage in a desert; and a widening gap between the salaries of presidents and the pittance paid to contingent teachers which is more and more in line with the spectrum of compensation observed in publicly listed corporations. None of this has occurred as a result of an imposition of formal requirements. Imagine then the consequences of a WTO trade regime which legally insists that regulatory standards, affecting procedures of accreditation, licensing, and qualification, might pose barriers to free trade in services.

By the time that GATS negotiations over education were initiated in 2000, the range of educational organizations that had established themselves overseas was already voluminous. These included 1) corporate spinoffs that do employee training and offer degrees such as Motorola University, McDonald Hamburger University, Microsoft's Certified Technical Education Centers, GE's Crotonville Colleges, Fordstar's programs, and Sun Microsystems' Educational Centers; 2) Private for-profit education providers like the Apollo Group, Kaplan Inc., De Vry and the mammoth Laureate Education group (which now owns higher education institutions all over South America and Europe, operates in over 20 countries, and teaches a quarter of a million students); 3) Virtual universities, like Walden University and Western Governors Virtual University in the U.S., the Learning Agency of Australia, India's Indira Ghandi National Open University, and the UK's Open University; 4) Traditional universities that offer distance learning, especially in countries like Australia and New Zealand where governments mandated the marketization of higher educational services in the 1990s; and 5) for-profit arms of traditional universities, like NYU's SCPS, or University of Maryland's University College, and eCornell.

In the years since then, the volume and scope of overseas ventures has expanded to almost every institution that has found itself in a revenue squeeze, whether from reduced state and federal support or skyrocketing expenses. As a result of market-oriented reforms in higher education, every one of Australia's public universities is aggressively involved in offshore education in Asia, creating a whole class of educational entrepreneurs, onshore and offshore, whose pursuit of monetary gain has inspired repeated calls for audits. Since many of these programs carry large fiscal risks, the tendency increasingly is to favor conservative models like franchising; producing syllabi in Australia to be taught entirely by local instructors offshore. There is not even a pretense of academic exchange involved in this arrangement; where education is little different from a manufacturing product designed at home, produced and assembled by cheaper labor abroad and sold to consumers in emerging markets. In the U.S. for-profit sector, entrepreneurs scrambling to meet overseas demand for degrees ("with no frills") that have an unambiguous market value, are taking advantage of notoriously loose accrediting procedures to set up shop and pitch their product. Lax regulation in some southern and western states, offshore diploma mill havens like St. Kitts and Liberia, or the infamous Sebroga, a small self-proclaimed principality in Italy, which has granted accreditation to dozens of dubious degree-granting entities, make it easy to license operators who open and close programs overnight to suit market demand.

With China's economy leapfrogging up the technology curve, the jumbo demand for high-value, professional-managerial talent there has sparked a goldrush with foreign universities scrambling to meet a need that the state (whose professed priority is to fund basic rural education) cannot. There are few US colleges which have not sent prospecting missions to China to scout out offshore opportunities in the last few years. As for their return on investment, many administrators come back from these trips pondering the lesson that foreign companies learned; it is not at all easy to make money in China, let alone break even, and least of all from a joint venture with a Chinese partner, which is the obligatory arrangement for most colleges. Even in the absence of guaranteed revenue, many will set up shop for the same reason that corporations have persevered there — to build their brand in the Chinese market or establish their name in the region in anticipation of a future windfall.

The United Arab Emirates and neighboring Qatar have been especially successful in attracting foreign colleges with lavish offers, and are engaged in a bidding war to outdo each other to add cultural cache to their portfolio of corporate brands; The Louvre, Sorbonne, and the Guggenheim were all approached by Abu Dhabi government representatives at roughly the same time NYU was asked to set up a branch campus. Dubai hosts a complex called Knowledge Village for offshore branch campuses from Pakistani, Russian, Canadian, and Indian, in addition to select British, Australian, and American universities, In Qatar, several top-brand American universities, including Carnegie Mellon, Cornell, Georgetown, Texas A&M, George Mason University, and Virginia Commonwealth, are already established in Doha's 2,500 acre Education City, with all expenses paid for by the royal family's Qatar Foundation.

Students in the Middle East have every reason to feel they may not be welcome in the U.S. after 9/11, while the philosophical world-view associated with the War on Terror has provided administrators with an additional set of arguments to justify their newfound presence in the region. Many of their faculty are no doubt persuaded by the Thomas Friedman-style reasoning that aspiring Middle Eastern students would be better served by a Western, liberal education than by the curriculum of a glorified maddrasseh. Never mind that the host countries in question are quasi-feudal monarchies that ruthlessly suppress Islamism, among other belief-systems, and are in no small measure responsible, as a result, for the flourishing of terror in the Middle East and beyond. So the debate falls along familiar lines — is it better to try to influence the political climate in illiberal societies by fostering collegial zones of free speech, or is the instinct to engage student elites in such societies a naive, or at worst, a colonial instinct?

Notwithstanding the rhetoric of any university's overseas mission, it is not at all easy to distinguish some of the new offshore academic centers from free trade industrial zones where outsourcing corporations are welcomed with a lavish package of tax holidays, virtually free land, and duty-free privileges. Indeed, in many locations, Western universities are physically setting up shop in free trade zones. In Dubai the foreign universities are basically there to train knowledge worker recruits in the Free Zone Authority's other complexes — Dubai Internet City, Dubai Media City, Dubai Studio City, DubaiTech, and the Dubai Outsource Zone. In Qatar, the colleges share facilities with the global high-tech companies that enjoy tax and duty-free investments under that country's free zone law. Some of China's largest free trade locations have begun to attract brand name colleges to relieve the skilled labor shortage that is hampering the rate of offshore transfer of jobs and technology. The University of Liverpool, first to open a branch campus in Suzhou Industrial Park (which attracts more FDI than other zone in the PRC), advertised entry-level positions at salaries beginning at $750 per month.

Corporate Universities?

Some readers might justifiably say that as long as the quality of education and integrity of research can be maintained, and the lure of monetary gain kept at bay, the push toward internationalization is something of a moral obligation for educators in affluent countries. Surely, it is a way of sharing or redistributing the wealth that the reproduction of knowledge capital bestows on the most advanced nations. Surely, the domestic hoarding of all this largesse only serves to perpetuate the privileges (not to mention the parochialism) of American students, while it sustains the grossly overdeveloped economy supplied by our universities. At a time when our multinational corporations are plundering the resources of the developing world in the scramble to patent genetic material and copyright indigenous folk tales, surely educators are obliged to set a better example.

In response, I would ask whether the overseas penetration of Anglophone colleges overseas is really the best way of delivering such goals, especially when the main impetus for expansion to date has clearly been less philanthropic than revenue-driven, and when the crisis of domestic student debt is more likely to be exported in the form of a new "debt trap" for students in developing countries to bear. Isn't there a more direct way for universities to make globally available the knowledge and research they generate?

One obvious alternative is to give it away for free, with no intellectual property strings attached. In MIT's pioneer OpenCourseWare project, the university makes its courses accessible online for self-learning and non-degree-granting purposes. Other colleges, like Tufts, Utah State, and Carnegie-Mellon have followed suit. To date, MIT's courses are being translated in China and other Asian countries. While laudable in inspiration, the content that is being imported has a clear cultural standpoint. If it is not absorbed alongside teachings from a local standpoint, it remains to be seen how this export model will differ, in the long run, from the tradition of colonial educations. All over the developing world, governments, desperate to attract foreign investment, global firms, and now, global universities, are channeling scarce public educational resources into programs tailored to the skill sets of a "knowledge society" at the expense of all other definitions of knowledge including indigenous knowledge traditions. Under these conditions, higher education is increasingly regarded as an instrumental training for knowledge workers in tune with capitalist rationality as it is lived within one of the urban footprints of corporate globalization.

If universities were to closely follow the corporate offshoring model, what would we expect to see next? In a labor-intensive industry like higher education (on par with the garment industry — 75% of education costs are the labor costs of instructors) employers will first seek to minimize the instructional budget, usually by introducing distance learning or by hiring local, offshore instructors at large salary discounts. Expatriate employees sent to set up offshore facilities become a fiscal liability to be offloaded at the first opportunity. Satellite campuses will be located in the same industrial parks as Fortune 500 firms, and will certainly be invited to produce customized research for these companies, again at discount prices. After a matter of time, an administrator will decide that it will be cost-effective to move some domestic research operations to the overseas branch to save money. And once the local instructors have proved themselves over there, they will be the ones asked to produce the syllabi and, ultimately, to teach remote programs for students back in the U.S.

Inevitably, in a university with global operations, administrators who have to make decisions about where to allocate its budgets will favor locations where the return on investment is relatively higher. Why build expensive additions at home when a foreign government or free trade zone authority is offering you free land and infrastructure? Why bother recruiting overseas students when they can be taught more profitably in their countries of origin? If a costly program can only be saved by outsourcing the teaching of it, then surely that is the decision that will be made. Along the way, there will be much high-minded talk about meeting the educational needs of developing countries, and some pragmatic talk about reducing the cost of education for domestic students. Substandard academic conditions will be blamed on foreign intermediaries or partners, or on "unfair" competition. Legislators and top administrators will grandstand in public, and play along in private. Clerical functions and data-dense research will be the first to go offshore. As for teaching instructors, those in the weakest positions or the most vulnerable disciplines will feel the impact first, and faculty with the most clout — tenured full-timers in elite universities — will be the last and the least to be affected.

As far as the domestic record goes, higher education institutions have followed much the same trail as subcontracting in industry — first, the outsourcing of all non-academic campus personnel, then the casualization of routine instruction, followed by the creation of a permatemps class on short-term contracts, and the preservation of an ever smaller core of full-timers, who are crucial to the brand prestige of the collegiate name. Downward salary pressure and eroded job security are the inevitable upshot. How do we expect offshore education to produce a different result?

From the perspective of academic labor, I don't believe we should expect an altogether dissimilar outcome. But the offshoring of higher education, if and when it occurs, will not resemble the hollowing-out of manufacturing economies, with full-scale employer flight to cheaper locations, or even the more recent select outsourcing of white-collar services, where knowledge transfer involves the uploading and downloading of skills and knowhow from and to human brains on different sides of the planet. The scenario for education will be significantly different, given the nature and traditions of the services being delivered, the vested commitment of national governments to the goals of public education, and the complexity of relationships between various stakeholders.

Moreover, for all the zealous efforts to steer higher education into the rapids of enterprise culture, it would be easy to demonstrate that, with the exception of the burgeoning for-profit sector, most universities do not and cannot, for the most part, function fiscally like a traditional marketplace, and that the principles of collaboration and sharing that sustain teaching, learning, and research are inimical or irreducible, in the long run, to financialization after the model of the global corporation. Yet one could say much the same about the organizational culture of the knowledge industries. High-tech firms depend increasingly on internationally available knowledge in specialized fields; they collaborate with each other on research that is either too expensive or too multi-sided to undertake individually; and they depend, through high turnover, on a pool of top engineers to circulate brainpower throughout the industry. So, too, the management of knowledge workers has diverged appreciably from the traditions of Taylorism, and is increasingly modeled after the work mentality of the modern academic, whose job is not bounded by the physical workplace or by a set period of hours clocked there. Modern knowledge workers no longer know when they are on or off the job, and their ideas — the stock-in-trade of their industrial livelihoods — come to them at any waking moment of their day, often in their most free moments. From this perspective, talk about the "corporate university" is a lazy shorthand. The migration of our own academic customs and work mentalities onto corporate campuses and into knowledge industry workplaces is just as important a part of the story of the rise of knowledge capitalism as the importation of business rationality into the academy, but the traffic in the other direction is all too often neglected because of our own siege mentality.

In all likelihood, we are living through the formative stages of a mode of production marked by a quasi-convergence of the academy and the knowledge corporation. Neither is what it used to be; both are mutating into new species that share and trade many characteristics. These changes are part and parcel of the economic environment in which they function; where, on the one side, a public commons unobtrusively segues into a marketplace of ideas, and a career secured by stable professional norms morphs into a contract-driven livelihood hedged by entrepreneurial risks; and, on the other side, where the busy hustle for a lucrative patent or a copyright gets dressed up as a protection for creative workers. Here the restless hunt for emerging markets masquerades as a quest to further international exchange or democratization.

It may be all too easy for us to conclude that the global university, as it takes shape, will emulate some of the conduct of multinational corporations. It is much more of a challenge to grasp the consequences of the co-evolution of knowledge-based firms and academic institutions. Yet understanding the latter may be more important if we are to imagine practical educational alternatives in a civilization which relies on mental labor to enrich its economic lifeblood.

Eurocentrism, the University, and Multiple Sites of Knowledge Production

Amit Basole

B y way of personal background, my first experience of university education was in the Biological Sciences. I received my bachelors and masters degrees (in microbiology and molecular biology) from the University of Bombay, India and my PhD in Neuroscience from Duke University in the US. Subsequently I switched ("followed my heart?") to Political Economy and am currently a PhD candidate in the Department of Economics at the University of Massachusetts, Amherst.

The central theme under discussion is "Conflicts in the Production of Knowledge." There are of course many important conflicts to understand and many different ways to understand these conflicts. The one between market-oriented and non-market-oriented teaching and learning (or alternatively between liberal versus vocational/professional education) is one that has been alluded to many times. Similarly the conflicts over greater democratization of the learning process, over open access to research and so on are also important. In my post I would like to take a somewhat different approach. The big questions that I am interested in are:

1. Can the European University (what I mean by this will become clear presently) show us a way forward out of the global socio-ecological crisis of late capitalism?
2. Further, in the context of post-colonial societies such as India, how can the modern university escape or transcend its Eurocentric origins and bounds and become more immediately relevant to society at large?

Needless to say, these are topics for entire research programs and here I can offer no more than discussion points (indeed I am not qualified to do much more). Instead of attempting to answer these directly I will raise related issues:

1. What are some of the contradictions/conflicts in the "European University" that stand in the way of it being a force for radical change?
2. In the post-colonial context, how can we think of the university in relation to the other sites where knowledge is produced in society?

The "European University": Contradictions

I realize that there is no such thing as "the University," there are only universities. However, today, as a result of European colonialism, universities in far-flung corners of the earth show some striking similarities. The most likely reason for this is not that, to take one example, economics, sociology, political science, anthropology and history are "natural" ways in which to divide the study of human society. But instead the reason we find these same "disciplines" in universities everywhere is because they are modeled on the "European University," a particular historical entity that arose in early 19th century Germany (Berlin), though of course antecedents are to be found in Paris, Bologna etc. [Note that this is not to say that "the university is a European idea," an unsurprising Eurocentrism that one often finds in historical accounts of the university, but only to point out that what we call the university today is modeled on an entity that arose in 19th Century Europe.] This much is perhaps commonplace. But what causes me to pose the question as above is that today I see the university — particularly in the post-colonial context, but also elsewhere — as a conservative force with a *status quo* bias, rather than as an agent of radical change. Let me explain.

Focusing on two main contradictions in the university, we find that the production of knowledge within the context of the disciplines allows for glaring contradictions of world-view to exist in the same site. There is no overarching ethical/moral principle that unites all disciplines. Should there be one? This is a matter for debate. I believe that lack of one makes possible the particular types of instrumental rationality that is rampant in science and engineering. Historically (prior to the fact-value separation which is the legacy of the European Enlightenment) this problem was solved by situating knowledge production in the religious context. Modern universities, in contrast either operate under a "knowledge for the sake of knowledge" dictum or even a more naked "knowledge for power" principle. Thus the only thing that unites English, Anthropology, Economics, Ecology and Engineering is that knowledge is produced there. So Anthropology can say we are all different while Economics says we are all the same, or Economics says capitalism can grow forever while Ecology says resources are limited or the English department can say we are all postmodern while Engineering displays all the features of modernist thought and so on. And these contradictions can not only exist, but they can be taught to students who are offered hardly any way to reconcile them (institutionally that is; I am not speaking of exceptions such as individual professors). Of course I am exaggerating the case somewhat to make a rhetorical point. The existence of "ecological economics" for example, shows that disciplinary cross-talk can happen. And such examples can be multiplied. However, the very term inter-disciplinarity tells us what takes primacy (disciplines) and what comes afterwards (inter). As has been pointed out, such fragmentation stands directly in the way of a coherent and holistic understanding of human society, its evils, its impact upon its environment and its likely future trajectory.

The second conflict or contradiction is the oft-repeated one between teaching and research, between knowledge production and dissemination. But still sometimes we forget that a university performs the function, not just of supporting professors and researchers but of training a far greater number of individuals to be something other than professors and researchers (I am referring of course to undergraduate students). Thus the university should be a place where ethically-guided, community-centered individuals are produced, who have acquired a holistic picture of human society and the problems it faces but who at the same time are technically or otherwise adept at their chosen trade or field. In other words engineers, builders and so on who are not instrumentally rational. Currently we do an excellent job of the technical training and leave the ethics to whoever cares to step up to the challenge. John Henry Newman begins his famous book *The Idea of a University* by defining the University as "a place for teaching universal knowledge." There are several keywords here that are of interest. We can take all of these in turn.

Before we begin, we must clarify of course that Cardinal Newman defends a model of the university that has been termed "pre-modern." Also it is clear that for Cardinal Newman, teaching is a more important function of the university, than what he calls "advancement," (or what we might call production) of knowledge. Why, he asks, would the university have students, if its primary purpose was knowledge production ("scientific and philosophical discovery")? The division of labor between knowledge production and dissemination envisioned by Cardinal Newman (teaching = universities, research = learned societies/academies) is of course no longer true (liberal arts colleges and research institutes represent this strict division of labor today, but the research university of course combines both). The tension between teaching and research embodied in the complaint that teaching leaves little time for research, is an all-too-familiar refrain at least in the natural science departments. But there is an even more significant conflict here. We live in times of super-specialization of disciplines when academic faculty often produce knowledge only for their peers and may even be punished via academic sanctions such as denial of tenure for not producing enough knowledge for specialist consumption (e.g. publishing newspaper articles to shape public opinion, rather than publishing in refereed journals). The more immediate impact upon society at large, of the university may therefore be, not knowledge produced in its research laboratories and its faculty offices, but the knowledge disseminated in its classrooms. In other words, shaping the worldview of students (and future participants in society's debates).

The multiplicity of knowledge production sites

Finally we come to the operative phrase in Cardinal Newman's sentence, universal knowledge. This conflict that has been mentioned several times on the Edu-factory list in the form of the debate on "multiple universalisms;" however I want to shift the terms of debate slightly and pose it as a question of the "multiplicity of knowledge production sites," the relationship between these sites and the related question of "serious" and "nonserious" knowledge. This is also tangled up (at least in my mind) with the conflict between Eurocentric and non-Eurocentric scholarship. Thus far from serving as an agent of emancipatory change, the university in the postcolonial context has often been an agent of "modernization" and university scholars, often the most "Westernized," have been generally dismissive of the knowledge produced in more "traditional loci" (or subaltern knowledge). The high academy has often slavishly followed European fashions and thinkers (be it deconstruction, post-structuralism, Foucault, Derrida or whatever) for their own sake (or to get published in Western journals). This has been true whether the university was neoliberal or not although things may be changing now. This is not to say that Foucault, to take one example, has nothing interesting to say in the context of India. But that is not a given fact. It needs to be evaluated.

As Rajesh Bhattacharya and I argue in "The Phantom of Liberty" (Kanth 2009), the lamentations often heard (e.g. from post-colonial scholars) that, for better or for worse, we are trapped within the confines of Eurocentric sociopolitical thought are often a result of the fact that we are taught to regard the academy as the (only?) legitimate site of knowledge production. We further argue that if one looks to other sites of knowledge production, non-Eurocentric analyses of society abound.

Post-colonial thinkers, in so far as they cannot think in their own language, are slaves of the master's discourse — or the master-discourse. What future can such a slave claim for herself? It must be understood that a "free" future for such a slave cannot be claimed solely by "Provincializing Europe" to borrow Dipesh Chakrabarty's phrase. It must also be accompanied by a retrieval of (lost) local wisdom and non-European intellectual traditions, be they elite or subaltern. Not only should the post-colonial scholar historicize and contextualize Marx and Weber, (s)he should be or feel enabled to read Gangesa and Abhinavagupta (two Indian thinkers quoted by Chakrabarty as examples of "inaccessible" authors.) Sadly, Chakrabarty cannot claim such a future. He even finds the project of provincializing Europe an impossibility.

> [S]ince "Europe" cannot after all be provincialized within the institutional site of the university whose knowledge protocols will always take us back to the terrain where all contours follow that of my hyper-real Europe — the project of provincializing Europe must realize within itself its own impossibility. It therefore looks to a history that embodies this politics of despair (Chakrabarty 2000, pp. 45).

Chakrabarty's despair is not only the result of the recognition of a loss in the past but a failure to imagine a "free" future. Hence his despair is a permanent state of being because salvation/redemption/freedom cannot be conceived outside Eurocentric boundaries. We assert that the post-colonial social scientists' failure to retrieve non-European discourses is a measure of their own inadequacy, a corollary of their insertion in the Western academic discourse. In order to be intelligible to the Western audience, in order to publish in Western journals, they necessarily have to speak within the framework circumscribed by Western thought-categories. Thus, the latter understandably becomes the only mode of thought 'available' to them. This has been the case, we argue, with postcolonial studies as well as subaltern studies. Even those who have discovered the original loss of language find it impossible to retrace the steps back to that incidence of momentous discursive violence. This is Thatcher's TINA ("There is no alternative!") in the sphere of social thought.

Further, even critiques of Eurocentrism which are expressed within the confines of the Global Academy, shaped and dominated as it is by the European intellectual tradition described above, are subject to what John Mowitt (2001) has called a "discursive price of admission." That is, even resistance to and protest against Eurocentrism has to be grounded in Western texts and authors so that it can be intelligible to referees of the global publishing circuits.

> Can we hope to publish in an international journal an article that refers primarily to vernacular texts, the majority of which might never be translated into major European languages?

Even if it gets published, the author will surely be criticized for citing obscure texts. Yet there is a sustained articulation of challenges to European modernity in many vernacular texts — in bad print and cheap jackets — published by small local Third World publishing houses. The "unavailability" of alternative non-European discourses reflects a materiality inherent in the discursive practices and institutions of global academia — a materiality that has the effect of screening out a large set of articulations, utterances, statements and cries as "non-serious" knowledge (Bhattacharya and Basole, 2009).

This brings up my next argument. I have said earlier that Eurocentric categories of thought have colonized our minds to such an extent that the many different processes of reproduction of our life are articulated and understood in the language of European modernity. Yet, resistance to the imperialism of categories exists too and exists everywhere, wherever such imperialism asserts itself, i.e. in all spheres of life. Consequently, counter-discourses emerge at numerous social sites, in the variety of social processes that constitute the postcolonial experience. These sites could provide radical alternatives to Eurocentric thought-categories — other ways of making sense of the world. These constitute an archive of "available" alternatives to European modernity.

Yet, most of us suffer from a fundamental elitism in contemporary social thought, which holds that knowledge is not produced at the site of living, where multiple processes of reproduction of life intersect; rather it is produced where life ceases to be alive, where human experience turns into dead raw materials to be intellectually processed into thought-categories, i.e. at the institutional location of the academia. We believe that there are multiple sites of knowledge production in a society, the academy being only one of them. Academic practices constitute a distinct social process. As a specific social process, it has a distinct institutional location or base (university, research institutes, journals and publishing houses), its unique rules of production and dissemination of knowledge statements (papers, conferences, university lectures, participation in the media as experts etc.) and its particular effect on other social processes (construction of meaning, production of world-outlooks etc.). But, most importantly, professional academia establishes its social status on the basis of a distinction between knowledge and non-knowledge and by claiming to be the sole site for production of "knowledge."

Perhaps one can allude here to Gramsci's famous quote that while all humans are intellectuals, not all perform the work of (professional) intellectuals. Although of course Gramsci is not concerned with the particular issue that we are dealing with here. Also note that our argument is not that professional intellectuals do not perform an important function in society. Indeed they do, however, that function a) obviously cannot be delinked from the position they occupy in the capitalist world-economy and culture (i.e. there are no universal intellectuals) and b) professional intellectuals (specific or otherwise) are not the only producers of knowledge, nor even "the most important" by whatever criterion.

Here the concept being developed at the Vidya Ashram in Varanasi becomes immediately relevant. This is the concept of "Dialogues on Knowledge in Society". The emphasis is not on conflict between the various knowledge production sites (universities, schools, monasteries and mosques, small businesses, ordinary life) which certainly exist, but instead on the possibility of engaging them in dialog with each other.

Bibliography

Bhattacharya, R. and Basole, A. "The Phantom of Liberty: Mo(der)nism and Postcolonial Imaginations in India," in Rajani, K. Kanth (ed) (2009), *The Challenge of Eurocentrism: Global Perspectives, Policy, and Prospects,* Palgrave Macmillan, Basingstoke.

Chakrabarty, D. (2000), *Provincializing Europe: Postocolonial Thought and Historical Difference.* Princeton University Press, Princeton.

Mowitt, J. (2001), "In the Wake of Eurocentrism: An Introduction." *Cultural Critique*, Minneapolis, v. 47.

Global Assemblages
vs. Universalism

Aihwa Ong

Through the Edu-factory discussion on knowledge and neoliberalism, an acknowledgement emerged that there are multiple universalisms.

I make two brief observations. First, as an anthropologist, I find the call to develop "common grounds" or "common values" stifling, almost as oppressive as the purported universalism of a neoliberal mode of knowledge production and management. A profound Euro-centric blindspot has not yet adjusted to the shifting global environment and relevance of other universalisms.

At stake in the discussion of the contemporary university is the notion of citizenship. We have long assumed that modern citizenship is based on European assumptions of a "universal subject" and a corresponding utilitarian notion of "the common good." Giorgio Agamben most recently revisited this universal conceptualization of humanity by invoking the ancient Greek distinction between *zoe* (sheer physical survival) and *bios* (an idealized realm of ethics and politics). However, such binarism in European discourses discount other kinds of universalizing moral discourses — e.g. the great religions — that pose alternative ethical norms of humanity.

The greatest difference between European and non-European conceptions of humanity is the difference in emphasis on individual and collective values. Asian ethical regimes in particular stress the centrality of ethics in shaping cultural and national identities. So while modern citizenship and the nation-state it refers to are global forms originating in the West, they become modified in diverse contexts of reception. We would do well to think not in terms of an assumed universalism, but of multiple ethical systems in play, i.e. ethical constellations.

My second observation is that universalizable technologies (capitalism, nation-state, citizenship) do not produce universalism or uniform planetary conditions, but rather specific assemblages of politics and ethics. Stephen J. Collier and I coin the term "global assemblage" to identify multiple, unstable constellations of universal and situated elements.

Particular sites (nations, cities, universities, etc.) are not merely transmission points for "exchanges," but nodes formed through the play of strategic power. The interplay of global and situated elements crystallizes situated conditions of possibility for the resolution of problems. There is no one-size-fit-all approach to problems of ethics and politics.

Avinash Jha notes rightly that the "university represented a particular resolution of the universal and the specific." Part of the work of professors would be to rethink our mega theories and help our students come to grips with a dynamic, heterogeneous world shaped by diverse constellations of ethics and politics, of citizenship and nation, of capital and culture. This approach may well be truly revolutionary in an academic culture that is so wedded to an unproblematic notion of universalism, and a disinterest in other worlds, other ethics, other solutions.

Finally, I would like to make one more note on other universalisms. Some elites in China are articulating a discourse of "other worldliness" (*biede sijie*) that we can gloss as an idiom of alternative modernity. Clearly, some people consider their version of the good life (enabled by knowledge production, etc.) as linked to their nation's emergence, and not an effect of "capitalist enclosure." Capitalist networks have helped opened up a previously isolated and backward nation, and there is widespread recognition of inequalities, exploitations and injustices proliferated through market relationships. Each year, tens of thousands of protests are mounted against land grabs by corrupt officials, but there is also massive support of the market's role in strengthening the Chinese nation. Oppressive power stems not only from the exercise of capitalist relationships, but more frequently from the exercise of political might.

This double or ambivalent perception of knowledge-driven capitalism is rather different than that of Western progressives who condemn capitalism as simply oppressive and destructive. As I mentioned before, instead of assuming a uniform condition of oppression, particular constellations or entanglements of markets, politics, and ethics shape the situated field of power, and thus the kinds of strategies in play. Universal formulations or actions are not always pertinent or helpful, and can worsen situations (e.g. US "pro-democracy" intervention in Iraq).

The differences among universalisms and situations articulating capitalism (e.g. neoliberal-authoritarian assemblages, or neoliberal-democratic-caste assemblages) pose a challenge to "commoning" practices. I think all of us support people having their own view of the good life and struggling to preserve cultural values and norms in the face of globalizing forces. Like all of us, they want to define and fight their own battles, and seek their own accommodations or changes. After all, in many situations, they have to pay for their ideals with their own lives.

Perhaps by commoning" we are refering to mutual respect, tolerance, and coexistence with diverse communities. It presupposes a genuine humanist concern and support for all peoples, but lacking the robust institutions of a world government, we should develop cross-cultural capacities for understanding particular situations, and for translating across diverse ethical regimes. A specific intellectual is by definition a situated cosmopolitan, at once particular and universal, anchored in her world and yet identified with other worlds.

Management of Knowledge
vs. Production of Knowledge
Sunil Sahasrabudhey

The unfolding reality of the last fifteen years is seen by us as a historic opportunity for the oppressed classes of the world, not because the Internet or the computer and communication technologies have appeared with a promise, but because they have unleashed a historic destabilization of world capitalism, concomitantly destabilizing both the university and the nation-state. The take over of the university by the corporations and of the national state by a trans-national state in the making, also called the Empire by American theorists, are the immediately visible phenomena. These have tended to put many of us on the defensive and if we are not careful we start defending the university and the state that capitalism had produced of which we are dissenting products.

The Internet has divided the world afresh into those who manage knowledge and those who produce knowledge. Conflicts in the knowledge domain constitute the gateway to an understanding of this phenomenon. These conflicts constitute the bed for the production of new theories that can produce new alliances, a new politics in the interest of the oppressed of the world. These conflicts of the knowledge domain are there in the fields, the workshops, the factories, in the riverbeds and forest terrains and also in the universities where people produce knowledge. The organization and manipulation of these knowledge-production activities is now managed over the Internet.

That the university is the chief location of the production of knowledge is the Euro-centric view. Theories of human emancipation, particularly emancipation of the oppressed, must see every human being as a knowledge producer.

Ordinary life in fact is that vast bed where knowledge is produced hourly, daily. Ordinary life is the life without condition. It presupposes no technology, no religion, no state, no university. People constantly produce new knowledge based on their genius, experiences and the needs of everyday life. There has perhaps never been a greater source of knowledge than ordinary life. I live in one of the most populous regions of the world. Here the life of the majority is just ordinary life. No air travel, no Internet, no electricity for half the day. Cities and towns are places of household artisanal production and small shops; the countryside is full of very small farmers. I trust different regions have different concepts of ordinary life and the majority everywhere is part of ordinary life. If we see this in a deprivation framework, we will be led to development theories; if we see this in an exploitation framework, we will be led to theories of radical social transformation.

Broadly speaking there are four locations of knowledge in contemporary society — University, Monastery, Internet and ordinary life. Science, religious knowledge, knowledge management and *lokavidya* are the chief occupants of these sites. (*Lokavidya* literally means "people's knowledge".) Knowledge management is in the process of assuming the command of the knowledge domain as much as information economy is assuming command in the domain of economics and a transnational state is situating national states as its subordinate and serving partners.

Production of knowledge in the monastery is minimal. Production of knowledge in the universities is in the process of splitting into two halves. One will become part of the activity in the Network Society and the other will be pushed down into the world of production, the world of technicians, artisans, farmers and forest dwellers. So part of the university will be gobbled up by the world of knowledge management and other parts will move to populate the already populated realm of ordinary life with its infinite variety of production of knowledge. What will happen to the university as an idea or as a campus reality I do not know; however, what appears to be staring into our faces is not the hitherto known division of society between managers of knowledge and producers of knowledge. The producers of knowledge are the oppressed classes and their seeing themselves as such is the condition of the politics of emancipation.

Knowledge management redefines what is knowledge: it aspires to be the knowledge itself. It does not represent only a new form or practice of management; rather it is primarily a new form of knowledge. We may deny it this status, and many do so, but knowledge management does occupy the top slot in the new knowledge hierarchy of the information age. It occupies the command position and rules from the virtual domain. Sitting at the top of the cyclone in the epistemic world it sucks in everything of substance. All knowledge that is produced anywhere feeds into it and all knowledge at the site of production stands emaciated and alienated. Knowledge producers thus enter into a fundamental conflict with knowledge managers. The transnational state develops primarily to manage this conflict. The American wars appear to underline the inherent irreconcilability of the situation. Only when producers of knowledge start understanding that their knowledge is turned against them in the new dispensation, the possibility of a new radical politics is born.

Short-Circuiting the Production of Knowledge

Nirmal Puwar and Sanjay Sharma

The interior and exterior space of the writer is blown up in Giancarlo Neri's *The Writer*; a thirty-foot table and chair made from six tons of steel, plated with wood and painted brown, and placed deliberately in Hampstead Heath (London, UK) in 2005, an area with a historical concentration of canonized writers (Keats, Freud, Marx, to name a few). As one moves around the elongated table legs and looks up from under the table, the weight of the world as it is carried by the labor of writers, overwhelms, tires and leaves one wondering. In the writing of the literary histories of this landscape we know that the processes of legitimation and memorialization have sliced out particular writers who have taken in the air of the heath and spoken out to the global currents of the landscape.

Only a five minute walk away from the sculpture, the house where C.L.R. James and George Lamming lived during the 1950s is located. The footprints of these Caribbean diasporic writers, as well as the scores of other theorists, musicians, students and writers from the colonies which have lived and written in the area are not part of the social imagination of what has been hailed as a specific literary corner of the world.

The guidebooks of local histories are not full of the concerns of C.L.R. James as he sat at his desk on 70 Parliament Hill writing about racism and revolt, for instance. Neither does the house have a blue plaque at the front of it. These blue circular memorial tablets are placed by English Heritage on buildings where people of eminence have resided or worked, they are one way in which visitors navigate the city. As the processes of consecration are rarely black/white and the conditions of inclusion are always uneven, there is nevertheless a blue plaque in a neighborhood nearby (Primrose Hill) to B. Ambedkar, a *dalit* political activist who fought against caste in India.

Countering exclusion and eurocentrism often produces an anxiety framed by content rather than grappling with the modalities of knowledge production. How often do we experience a bemusement amongst academic colleagues when they implore "there just aren't enough minority or third world concepts, writers, and theorists on our programmes!," or repeatedly ask "what or who should be included in the curriculum?" This kind of accretive multicultural model naively pluralizes knowledge and fails to take on what pedagogy is — a contested process of knowledge production. And nor does it properly grasp what knowledge can do — mobilizing unruly connections and ways of becoming otherwise. What gets labelled as multicultural knowledge has to be refigured in relation to the emergence of a particular cultural formation — how an identity or knowledge of "otherness" is constituted. To encounter and produce "non-Eurocentric" knowledge means at least questioning how systems of colonial governance and knowledge have jostled to maintain a manichean divide between the same-other, west-rest while desiring/disavowing the multicultural.

The conditions in which a particular culture, identity or knowledge emerge, and the constant negotiations, dissonant exchanges, and operations of power which inscribe particular differences need to underwrite our pedagogies. Cultural difference cannot be reduced to the consensual unity or the banality of pluralized knowledges. Rather, the multicultural inhabits the entangled political terrain of possibly discordant and disruptive cultural encounters. To practice pedagogy means risking antagonistic exchanges in a classroom, and with incommensurable points of view and knowledges not being diffused in the moment of their expression.

The questions "what is knowledge for?" and "what does knowledge do?" cannot be answered in their generality. Likewise, as Stuart Hall pointed out many years ago, there are no pedagogies in general. This doesn't suggest we simply valorize the local, whether as a counter to the charge of eurocentrism, or champion specificity as an antidote to hegemony of the universal. The pursuit of the particular — for example, in the demands separate Islamic, Sikh, Jewish schooling in the UK or ethnic studies in the USA — often leads to a reductive mode of identity politics bearing suspect claims of cultural authenticity on behalf of racialized groups.

It is hardly surprising that neoliberal education is embracing cultural difference for an ever-expanding multicultural capitalism. Certain kinds of (acceptable) fragmented subjectivities are at the very heart of a new culture-knowledge economy. Knowledge about otherness — ways of life, cross-cultural hybridities and geographies, emerging markets, technologies and communications — has become vital to producing a new information-rich, self-reflexive, educated class for the needs of transnational capital. Moreover, when a student is more interested in maximizing their grades rather than immersing themselves in critical thinking and analysis, is this a failure of radical pedagogy or merely symptomatic of a world out there that is already operating within everyday university teaching? Increasingly, we find ourselves equipping students with skills to successfully compete as flexible workers in an age of neoliberal governance. However much we individually pursue a reflexive micropolitics of knowledge in our teaching, a disciplinary curriculum driven by market imperatives and standardized assessments is not easy to institutionally challenge and transform. The collective, dialogic pedagogies in the early work of the Birmingham Centre for Contemporary Cultural Studies (CCCS) appear for instance, anachronistic today.

An association with the writers block is one of the intended points of attention of the sculpture for Neri, of course each engagement with the piece is able to produce much more. Perhaps though, proliferation rather than block has become the condition of writers including academics, who now know the judicious statement *publish or perish* only too well. A continuous lattice of works keeps the spider's web of writing spinning. For the global 'A'-list stars of academia a book a year seems to have increasingly become the bench mark annual speed of production. As we invent and produce more books, blogs, video clips, podcasts, e-lists and sub-sub-specialist journals, as well as generating multiple variations on Centres and degree programs, proliferation has become a means of existing.

The art of reinvention keeps the masters at bay, showing that you are at the forefront leading the latest game in town, while at the same time allowing us to create MySpace, a 24-hour generator of "novel" ideas for the curriculum, research and administration. Reinventing education through experimentation and novelty allows old time radicals to play around with chairs and squares — some how shifting the architectures of power? The finely tuned MySpace functions as a social and emotional magnet and hub, offering some scope for autonomy and reigns over the levers of the educational regimes we inhabit and produce, with desire and longing. At the same time the sinking funds of institutions and departments remain a constant driver for niche marketing universities, courses, as well as the self, of course. University promotion procedures hinge on evidence of both generalist management skills as well as ingenuity in assessment methods, sub-sub disciplines, student recruitment targets, you name it. We all know that the international market (the double, trebled fees of "there" coming over "here") affords continuous flexibility and invigilation of targeted zones on the world map and methods of global contact.

Diverse, competing and overlapping transnational circuits of knowledge production and exchange are in process. Local, Eurocentric, capitalist, postcolonial academies and academics are all inside this. However we know that positionality is central and not secondary to the commodification process, points of entry are unequally experienced, just as sustainability is. Neither does proliferation of international contacts and exchanges of different orders and scales mean that the consecrated methods of induction and inculcation of *Homo Academicus* have fallen away. The academic tribes simultaneously exercise reproduction while being flexible to reinvention. The strength of social cloning and tacit endorsement procedures continues through the academic machinery. Doublespeak in terms of devotion to radical theories of flow, percolation, assemblages, syncretic fusions, border dialogues and re-terroritorialisation live alongside the exercise of Jesuit methods of recruitment. The market, status and recognition subsist in this world together.

"Representations of an Intellectual," the published Reith Lectures that Edward Said delivered at the invitation of BBC (1993), eloquently grapples with the role and the style of the public intellectual. A loud chorus had objected to Said being the chosen presenter for these prestigious annual public lectures, on the grounds that, because of his politics in the Middle East, he was not a proper intellectual of the ilk and quality worthy of this honorable position of authority. Thinking of the distinctive signature of an intellectual, and while having issue with the texture of the intellectual as "a dreary moralistic preacher," he smokes out "the insiders, experts, coteries, professionals" who often comprise "a superior little band of all-knowing men in power." He highlights the "intellectuals' relationship with institutions (academy, church, professional guild) and with worldly powers, which in our time have coopted the intelligentsia to an extraordinary degree," while urging a sense for texture and flare in the enactment of the public responsibility. We could undoubtedly ponder on how Said's own somatics of speech, habitus and authority, as a postcolonial intellectual, offered him entry to the inside, while not being quiet right, as far as the bestowal of invitations, honors and blue plaques are concerned. In addition, it is also worth paying attention to how even the critical experts of academia invest in coteries and professional identifications that result in unproductive schisms which scream and claim outsider or insider status.

Thwarting the simplistically positioned Eurocentric, modernist, post-colonialist, class camps and categories of comfort, in an international exchange, right from within the academy, Edward Said, as the President of the Modern Language Association (MLA), invited Pierre Bourdieu to present a keynote address to the association. On a satellite link from Paris to Chicago, Bourdieu argued for a scholarship of *commitment,* "the productions of critical networks that bring together specific intellectuals (in Foucault's sense of the term) into a veritable collective intellectual capable of defining by itself the topics and ends of its reflections and action — in short, an autonomous collective individual...It can organize or orchestrate joint research on novel forms of political action, on new manners of mobilizing and making mobilized people work together, on new ways of elaborating projects and bringing them to fruition together."

Mainstream accounts of the intellectual trajectory of Bourdieu are notable for their occlusion of his colonial/post-colonial formation and connections. This is perhaps not surprising given that the Algerian connections of Durkheim, Levi-Strauss, Althusser, Derrida and Cixous, are rarely central to investigation of these social theorists. For Bourdieu, his time in Algeria during the French occupation (on conscription and then as a lecturer), continued to impact upon him throughout his years. Before his sudden death, he had started to curate an exhibition with Franz Schultheis (President of the Bourdieu Foundation, Geneva) and Christine Frisinghelli (Camera Austria, Graz) from the hundreds of photographs he had taken while he was in Algeria. Aside from a few that appeared on his books, the bulk of the photographs remained in a shoe-box, although he regularly took them out and reflected on them. The photos were field notes for him as well as being therapeutic aids for coping with the violence of 3 million displaced by French pacification policies. He was drawn towards what he observed as the art of invention in impossible situations.

At Goldsmiths, we have installed the 150 photographs of the touring exhibition within the university campus for this academic year. Notwithstanding the industrial tendency of academic fandom, for us, inhabiting the exhibition offers the possibility of raising and working through a number of questions:

- of how social thought has been cooked up in colonial and postcolonial encounters
- of the place of academics and intellectual work in war time
- of the modes of cultural translation and transformation.

Of note is how a pedagogy of representation of Bourdieu's photographs throws into sharp relief what is constructed as European/non-European knowledge production. To insert Bourdieu into a post-colonial frame of reference neither simply turns to the locality of Algerian otherness (as a radical "outside" space of Europe), nor utilizes otherness merely as an ontological category for deconstructing the origins of Europe. While Bourdieu's photographic practice eschewed dominant colonial regimes of representation, arguably he remained governed by traces of Orientalism. Nevertheless, the exhibition of his work opens up the opportunity to mobilize other ways of knowing. And it is this short-circuiting of the hegemony of racialized knowledges which activates the possibility of an ethics of difference.

Conditions of Interdisciplinarity

Randy Martin

Interdisciplinarity appears under so many guises it might seem to be the organizing universal within the university. And yet, every utterance of the term betrays a certain parochialism. While the speaker is often located in a western research university, the rarefied address is taken as representative of some generic academic home. Given its proliferation, the conditions of interdisciplinarity are at once general and particular, mandated from above and driven from below, everywhere recognizable and differently sited. It is perhaps then wisest to hold the tension between work that emerges within a given institutional setting and the range of intellectual projects that transcend location. While there are any number of dimensions that establish a given interdisciplinary moment, the accretion of historical factors can be arrayed into formations that vary occupationally, institutionally, organizationally, geopolitically, and epistemologically. This highly differentiated space is not simply a backdrop upon which to map an instance of academic labor. Rather, the work undertaken entails an active shuttling between spaces, a series of lateral moves that demand attention to what expertise travels and what is left behind as we move from the places of disciplinary formation to those disparate events of reception. These circumstances adhere to my own biography. My professional training is in sociology, but also the performing arts. In addition, I've spent ten years in academic administration, first as the chair of a department (staffed by variously identified social scientists and historians) that created a program in cultural studies, and more recently as an associate dean of faculty and interdisciplinary programs. For intellectual audience and interlocutors, I've often turned to the humanities as a kind of bridge between the arts and social sciences. These experiences have provided the opportunity to devise several curricular initiatives, and to address my own research (which ranges from performance as a lens to grasp the political, to the cultural economy of personal finance and the use of risk management in war) to a variety of audiences. The traffic in interdisciplinarity makes one keenly aware of how situational its terms of knowledge production can be. Conferences, guest lectures and seminars accrue as a global currency that trades an imagined outside based on some measure of reputation and institutional subvention for local needs that the occasion is meant to articulate. While giving a seminar with a museum curator to a group of artists interested in policy questions, one participant invoked the need for social science expertise to ask how better assessment design might help assure the efficacy of her project. The question was intelligently formulated, yet addressed to someone who would want to make assessment self-critical so as to scrutinize those kinds of demands for legitimacy. In this case the social sciences were being asked to deliver positive knowledge to artists that would render the terms of exchange unproblematic. One week later, I participated in a meeting on financialization, a neologism that references the dominance of financial logics in business and daily life. The organizers had skillfully brought to the table what they took as the two most salient streams of research in political and cultural economy. The presentations were all quite lively, yet the divide persisted and was characterized by the key organizer as between those who did the systemic analysis and those who engaged political questions. In this taxonomy it was, ironically, the cultural economists who were deemed to undertake the latter kind of work. In both examples, interdisciplinary knowledge is articulated in what Mary Louise Pratt has called in a different context, a "contact zone" where the global and universal are reinscribed for a particular otherness that closely resembles disciplinary authority.

As labels are wont to do, these sit uneasily. Interdisciplinarity can claim little novelty in the fissure between naming and reference. What is more striking in these two examples is that they convene an array of recognizable differences in position and background but underwrite a more comprehensive kind of partition, what in the social sciences amounts to a sorting of worldly affairs into politics, economics and culture. The conceptual utility of these three terms as distinguishing between social processes of regulation, production, and lived experience seems almost inescapable (imagine the difficulty of thinking about the world without them). Yet this trinity quickly becomes holy when it is used to describe physically discrete locations within society or distinct categories of knowledge with mutually exclusive categories of expertise. Hence, while all sorts of disciplinary boundaries are getting blurred, the underlying epistemic delineations remain untouched. Not only are aspects of the social world unduly segregated, but the question of how the architectures of knowledge reanimate practical interventions in that world become severely circumscribed. The cautionary note here is that if interdisciplinarity stands as some kind of generic boundary-blurring, more than the presumed progressive value of blurring goes unthought. A more durable and obdurate set of positions and assumptions may remain unreflected upon in a way that ultimately compromises the ability to achieve the specific goals of the work in question.

How then to attend to this antinomy between a highly dispersed particularity and an unspoken or ungoverned universality? Rather than begin with its default universality, interdisciplinary work may get farther by starting within its own limitations. Two projects I have been involved with are worth mentioning in this regard. One involves a core curriculum at the Tisch School of the Arts, New York University. The very idea of a core is enough to agitate allergies from any number of quarters. The hubris involved in efforts to establish what is asserted to lie at the center of an educational mission, and the accompanying conviction that faculty and students will be left in a position to do their most effective teaching and learning has crashed many interdisciplinary vessels. The curricular location of the Tisch core tempts these fates. It partners the art school faculty and graduate students with the University's program in expository writing. Plenary lectures taught by senior faculty are paired with small writing sections staffed by non-permanent full time lines. But some aspects of the curricular design countervail convention. The large lecture functions more as a recitation section in the strong sense of the term — here ideas are rehearsed and students must figure out how to attend to the work of composition, for the professor essays visual material and shares techniques for assembling an argument. The evaluated writing is done in the smaller sections. The large lecture is not a center but an instance of a public sphere, as the students are invited to consider themselves public intellectuals on behalf of the arts with the essay work engendering the kind of voice required to represent and open a space for the arts in a world often hostile to it. These strategies worked out in the university setting for thinking about the encumbrances of professional communities for civic action and engagement we term artistic citizenship. Unlike its national cognate, artistic citizenship is partial in the double sense of committed and non-exhaustive. Instead of beginning with the stable mimesis of whole person and universal interest of the world, students are asked to reflect on how they generalize themselves from their given productive and contingent position as artists and professionals.

A second project is the creation of a new graduate program in arts politics. The aim of the program is to convene a space for activists where questions of what art and politics are is kept open. While the university is typically appealed to as possessing a monopoly of legitimating knowledge by virtue of its capacity to grant professional credentials, this program is post-professional in that it invites those already doing critical work to return to the university to elaborate the significance of their involvements and consider how they fit within a larger pantheon of possibilities. The idea is to join artists, scholar-critics, and those working in the institutional fields of art (even if these are aspects of the same person), in a conversation with a strategic and planning focus. The conceit of the program is the premise that far from a crisis in art or politics, we face a crisis of critical evaluation that minimizes the way we think about the efficacy of our own contributions, thereby rendering them more difficult to sustain. Students need to come with a project in mind and leave with a plan for intervention that changes its terms and conditions. The planning process for this program initially drew some scepticism from other schools as to the appropriateness of housing an intellectually based program in an art school. The program was initially designated "cultural politics" in reference to its most proximate epistemic domain. The concerns from various quarters had the effect of condensing the name and focusing the program, hence arts politics and a partnership among five schools and some two dozen faculty.

The circulation back into the university, long a feature of professional programs, poses an interesting challenge to the historically occidentalist claims of education as an ends in itself by which the liberal arts have positioned themselves. This boundary blurring of the university itself stands as a strong externality for the formation of interdisciplinarity. The humanities have often positioned themselves as the defenders of this particular boundary, given that its transgression often brings a rush of market values into a vibrant scene of resistance to them. This position has been eloquently defended by Mary Poovey, who invites a reinvestment in the human as a strategy for both refusal and self-preservation. As she puts it:

> The only way we can evaluate the effects of market penetration into the university in terms other than the market's own is to assert some basis for evaluation that repudiates market logic and refuses market language. In order to assert an alternative basis for evaluation, we must establish a normative definition of this alternative that is just as tautological as the logic of the market. For the purposes of discussion, I want to call this normative alternative "the humanities." I do so not because disciplines in the humanities necessarily or inevitably perform the function of critique, but because, as the sector of the university least amenable to commodification, the humanities may be the only site where such an alternative might survive.

The alternative amounts to asserting the existence of non-quantifiable "goods in themselves" which means to "risk something that post-structuralism has taught me to abhor: I have to essentialize 'the human.'" Poovey's strategy is to specify a unique normative function for the humanities. "The function of the humanities in the university is to preserve, nurture, analyze, interrogate, and interpret this living body of cultural materials.... In order to realize this norm, humanities disciplines would have to endorse a model of knowledge that does not emphasize utility, accumulation or progress...." Because "the humanities have no market worth" their "lack of economic potential may be the only asset capable of insulating us from market logic."

Poovey's arguments help us think strategically about the positioning of the humanities within the university. What is typically grounds for defensiveness, namely that the humanities have not been at the forefront of fresh revenue streams for the resource-hungry institution, are here made a virtue. Both the lack of economic potential and the irreducibility of the living body of cultural materials to the economic logics of quantification and accumulation provide the humanities with their distinct rationale for continued support. Poovey's situational essentialism recalls Gayatri Spivak's notion of strategic essentialism. Both intend to consolidate a position of value so that further political engagement can take place. If the humanities emerge here as a distinct asset, it is not without conceptual cost that is particularly relevant to interdisciplinary work. For if culture is enclosed and encapsulated against something outside it called the economic, or conversely if the economic is something outside of the living body referenced by culture, the ambit of what the humanities might be able to preserve is greatly diminished. This loss would establish a brief for an interdisciplinary project to which Poovey herself has contributed mightily — namely, the culturalization of economic logics.

In a different way, it is hard to sustain the claim that the humanities as an institutional formation are somehow less caught up in university business-models. Humanities core curriculum requirements have themselves provided templates for casualization, outsourcing, contingent graduate student labor, and a variety of other schemes by which norms of accumulation have been installed in the university irrespective of the putative content of the field. A strategy of resistance that takes as stable the delineation between instrumental and substantive reason, between the administrative form and content of knowledge, may not be able to track the critical difference which the knowledge might actually make to the organization of the university. While the humanities can (and must) be conceived as an intellectual project, they are never free of their institutional instantiation which renders them an administrative category as well. Why the humanities are better placed strategically to resist market logics than critiques of the market that can be found across all disciplines, is a matter of political discovery and not definitional fiat. Certainly the knowledge required to critique what markets are doing inside and outside of higher education require an interdisciplinary energy that is not served by an acceptance of the trinitarian partition of knowledge into humanities, social sciences and natural sciences. These architectural principles are not robust enough to organize the alliances or provide the knowledges that are most urgent for the very circumstances that Poovey so aptly identifies as the common predicament of the university.

If the humanities themselves cannot provide a sufficient bulwark against commodification, it may be that they themselves have become unmoored from their foundational purpose of the sort that Poovey describes, or that any interdisciplinary initiative simply gets coopted by the content-leaching actions of the university's administrative machinery. Such are the forceful arguments that Bill Readings offers in his diagnosis of the university of excellence. Excellence for Readings is a compulsive comparison without reference to the interior substance that fleshes out knowledge, "a unit of value internal to a system, the elemental unit of a virtual scale." Excellence reduces the aims of all endeavors to the outcomes of external evaluations as measured by quantitative ranking. The idea of living in a ruin is that we no longer inhabit a continuous history of progress. Unlike Poovey, the loss of progress does not preserve culture, but rather displaces the cultural in favor of excellence. "Once the notion of national identity loses its political relevance, the notion of culture becomes effectively unthinkable." An interdisciplinary project like cultural studies becomes symptomatic of this loss. One irony of Readings account is that the ruining of the university that forces it outside of its privileged relation to historical continuity itself rests upon a kind of historicizing narrative. Once upon a time national culture was intact and the humanities anchored its identity. The university was the key edifice of this constructive endeavor. The rise to predominance of the transnational corporation is the principal force behind the erosion of national culture. The university itself is consequently converted into this form.

Readings certainly provides a report from the front when the din of excellence and accountability threatened to wipe out all other conceptions of what the university might be. Without doubt, excellence continues to make a lot of noise. Readings also offered an oppositional politics within the university, "the question of value becomes more significant than ever, and it is by raising value as a question of judgement that the discourse of excellence can be resisted." If the university is to become a site of obligation and ethical practice it must answer to the question of justice not truth. It remains open to dispute, including to matters of accountability that cannot be reduced to accounting. Readings invites university presidents to spend more time reading faculty evaluations rather than pursuing measures of excellence. His analysis is prescient, but ten years on excellence is hard to disguise as a rhetoric of fundraising, a course that consumes the time of presidents and many others.

But this is not a change in the function of the president, but rather the demographics of the student and donor population from which funds are drawn. Diversity signals an abstract market to which a campus must establish a product niche, bringing a corporate identity to the scene of a former community constituency (on the basis of religion, gender, race, geography). And yet by centering the transformation of the university in the humanities, other operations of the university are elided. The university becomes transnational and its mission shifts from cultural identity to excellence in a way that preserves the insularity between what is inside and outside the university. The pressures for the reproduction of certain kinds of labor have long been reflected in the university curriculum, as has the intricate relationship with the business establishment. Whether or not there was a time when national culture was intact and effectively reproduced through a disciplinary structure, narrating the university as if this were its hegemonic ideal greatly simplifies the very political economy and class relations that Readings wants us to attend to in the present incarnation of the institution. The rise of professional schools have been just as much a feature of the emergence of the modern university and these have been quintessentially formations of transnational capital flows. The advent of professional geography, so effectively documented by Neil Smith, has been essential to the imperial sweep of the university in the world. Ultimately, the positing of an externality like the nation, against which the university rises and falls circumscribed other imaginings of the work available to us that might make interdisciplinarity serviceable to more than formal schemas of self-replication.

Once we recognize that the humanities are more effective when pluralized than when they stand consolidated as a singular institutional or epistemological formation, it becomes possible to rethink the boundaries of what is considered inside and outside the university. In his potent revisionist account of the relation between business and the humanities, Christopher Newfield has accomplished exactly this reconsideration. He grasps well the imbrication of both commerce and culture and the university with the economy as both a historical foundation and a basis for political intervention. As he puts it:

> I was thus not searching for literary and cultural study that existed outside of capitalist economics. I also thought that commerce as such was not only inevitable but also good, since it was at bottom a central form of human exchange and of mutual aid. I was morally opposed to core elements of capitalist commerce: its enormous inequalities, its exploitation of so much labor, its consistent conflicts with democracy, all of which seemed to be getting worse. At the same time, capitalism's large organizations and orchestrated workforces

wrought daily miracles of invention, production, and distribution. The forces of innovation and transformation that I
loved in the humanities appeared in different and often cap-
tive and yet impressive forms in the modern corporation.
Both locations — the corporation and the university — spon-
sored the true wonder of sociable, even socialized creativity.

The parallel and intersecting logics allow the humanities — properly
conceived — to play a key role in the reconfiguring of the relation between
the economy and its organizations, where the university itself is a key expression. The hybrid form can be understood as managerial humanism.
"Within this culture, generations of university staff and students learned to
stress self-development and to see the economic system as functionally prior
to their individual activity and uninfluenced by it." The sociological expression of this phenomenon was the rise of the professional-managerial class
(PMC), which treated administrative labor as a kind of craft legitimized by
the credentials of expert academic training. Humanism itself, according to
Newfield, is uninflected ethically and politically — it can just as readily subvert as advance emancipatory possibilities. As such, he emphasizes the tradition and trajectory of radical humanism. "The radical humanist regarded
managerial systems as the product of collaborative labor rather than as predetermined social system, one that could be remade if necessary. The radical humanist insisted that the PMC recognize and use its own agency within
expert systems as it emerges from its everyday work."

As with the market and the nation, the PMC is an external social formation that exerts pressures on the university. Yet in Newfield's account,
this class formation is made possible by and drives the expansion of higher
education. He also understands well that what was initially a vessel of class
mobility becomes a medium of social stratification. By 1980, "Professional
and managerial practices no longer seemed to seek meaningful independence from markets and finance. The PMC had virtually ceased to exist as a
separate interest in society. Its upper strata formed a classic bourgeoisie,
while those downstairs managed employees...The research university was as
important as business and government in engineering these compromises."
The braiding of professional autonomy and disciplinary expertise both pre-
served values of freedom and cast them as recidivist with respect to contemporary economic development. The middle class came to both distrust
and preserve its craft impulses even as it lost the privilege associated with
these prerequisites of professional entitlement. "Modernity, through the university, became the condition in which the middle classes were convinced
that non-instrumental thought and work have been exhausted. Economic de-

terminism and other symptoms of modernity arose from the PMC's loss of belief in the historical agency of all members of a culture, themselves included, which in turn flowed from the dissociation of craft and management, of art and the social processes of organizations."

By refashioning the middle class along self-managerial lines, the university abetted a broader social transformation toward a political economy of risk that accompanied the predominance of finance in organizing business and culture. The social compact being refigured by the Reagan revolt augured a shift from defined benefit entitlements and social security to the defined contribution approach to personal financial investment through tax-deferred savings and mutual funds. The corporate emphasis on shareholder value or boosting market price as against overall growth in capacity was a cognate of the shift from Keynsian to monetarist economic policy. The Keynsian program used citizenship-driven benefits of increasing wages and government expenditure to assure steady economic growth. Monetarism shifts the policy emphasis to minimizing inflation which is anathema to participation in financial markets — for it erodes the predictable gains of long-term investments and undermines calculation of market tendencies. While the Keynesian compact privileges the consumptionist notions of belonging to an American Dream that underwrote middle class ascendancy, the monetarist policy program focuses on the investor's willingness to undertake risk. Rather than being inside or outside the security of the middle class, populations are sorted between the risk capable and the at-risk those able to manage credit and debt for personal gain and those whose inabilities to do the same threaten national competitiveness.

This was the argument of a key domestic policy document, "A Nation at Risk," which applied accountability norms to education. The idea that individual performance and productivity rather than civic participation was the means and ends of education transformed the university experience from a public to a private good. Defunding of grants and aid in favor of greater debt loads was presented as a more rational allocation of resources if a degree correlated with lifetime value-added income capacity. Those denied security became a menace to society to be policed by a series of wars. The wars on crime, drugs, youth, culture and art not only metaphorized an enemy within, but normalized combat against the "at-risk" along the lines of a military campaign prosecuted by federal institutions. The war on terror is but the most recent legacy of these policy shifts from mass security to risk management. Rather than saving for a future that will deliver a utopian dreamscape free from toil, the embrace of risk brings the future into the present in an anticipatory or preemptive mode. This is the policy attitude of adjusting interest rates to combat prospective inflation and of the forward deterrence exhibited by recent military interventions by the United States in Afghanistan and Iraq.

The financial logic being described here does not curtail the demographic expansion of the PMC, or other entailments of middle class life like home ownership and college education. While these key indicators of belonging to the PMC continue to rise, its utopian promise of freedom and its historic project of expert autonomy run aground. Through such organizational vehicles as health maintenance organizations and internal auditors (of the sort made notorious by ENRON) professional occupations have lost ownership over their conditions of practice and become proletarianized. Yet the professional orientation in higher education incorporates the rising percentage of professional degrees over those in the liberal arts, and also the professional orientation of many liberal arts fields themselves. The professional turn that brings the outside of the university within has also propelled the reorganization of academic labor from the supreme security system — tenure — to a risk model of casualized part-time and now full-time faculty appointment. Real-world experience is embraced against a putative parochialism of the exclusive academic resume as if the professor is always applying for their own job. Academic entrepreneurialism accommodates changes in patent law that make universities closer to factories for intellectual property that convert forays in shareholder value into Readings-like quests for excellence. The culture wars treat critical intellectuals as placing national cultural literacy at risk by calling into question the interest served by this national account. Interdisciplinarity is assigned suspicion before its evidence can be heard that academic expertise lacks credibility. Ironically, the very postmodernism said to be the province of the accused is a tactic of accusation that authorizes doubt regarding the legitimacy of self-policing professionals. The Hippocratic oaths of the professionals to do no harm are replaced with a demand that shareholder benefit be demonstrated in every academic utterance or intellectuals will be lambasted for a nefarious speech act that has them possessed by demon-seeds.

Interdisciplinarity figures this double crisis of professional labor and disciplinary authority in a manner consonant with the larger economy of risk. But interdisciplinarity also offers a different model of academic labor, a collaborative one that has the potential to reorient work when the new university disavows the labor that it relies upon. What is conventionally offered to faculty as their fulfillment of the university's higher monastic calling by means of service, is more properly understood as administration. That service is both devalued for material concerns like merit pay, and elevated as sheer ideological faith in the rightness of the enterprise, speaks to the mischievous role it plays in diverting strategic reflection on the work involved in directing the course of university life. The contribution of interdisciplinarity in turn, can be to identify what the entanglements of risk hold for academic labor. The volatility visited upon academic life is not only destructive of relative security and freedom, it also embodies approaches to the mutual indebtedness by which risk circulates and expands. Leveraging the flows, alliances, movements of inside and outside positions interdisciplinarity as a kind of arbitrage, an investment in small fluctuations in value to greater effect.

The financialization of society in general and the university in particular has proceeded too far to stand apart from the entanglements of risk. To seek unsullied ground as a defense against baleful developments invites a kind of victimhood. Doubtless, while the reconciliation of labor along the lines of ascendant capital formations induces its own forms of nausea, there is also some prospect for significant political responses if we rethink value along the lines of the derivative, which counts as capital's own most generative investments. For capital, the derivative is a means of generating commensurability among entities that are different from one another so that risks are both dispersed and brought to market. Presently denominated at nearly $400 trillion in promissory notes and contracts, the profusion of derivatives enlarge the scope of mutual indebtedness and the volatility by which a move at one point ripples elsewhere. As such it is a worthy figure to think through the fateful combinations of universalisms and particularities. Derivatives take myriad forms, but are contracts that allow for exchange at certain terms at particular moments, like an agreement to trade currency at a fixed rate on a certain date (a future), or the opportunity to swap a contract to buy stock at different prices keyed to disparate market conditions (a swaption). Interdisciplinarity is also a currency whose value is derived, whose combinations are open, and whose effects can circulate extensively through relatively modest investments. The mutual indebtedness borne by interdisciplinarity carries no guarantees. At its most retrograde, it can isolate scholars of color, postcoloniality and heteronormativity to perform compensatory acts of representation for the institution's lack of commitment to diversity under impossible conditions of labor by which appointments are split and committee work multiplied. It offers a very different way of valuing academic labor and thinking about how epistemological and institutional formations intersect according to various organizational strategies. In order to amplify the strategic possibilities of interdisciplinarity at this conjuncture, it is important to think of an interdisciplinary history by which we can begin to forge a habitable future.

In the history of interdisciplinarity — like so many other histories — social forms and forces get introduced but nothing ever seems to fully disappear. For that reason it may be more useful to imagine waves that continue to break upon a shore of the present, rather than of periodization by which a singular tendency ends and another comes into view. That said, we can consider three interdisciplinary waves, all of which leave their residues on the present in terms of occupational, disciplinary and organizational formations, as well as responding to and internalizing various externalities. Sketching the matrix of these possibilities restates the arguments already presented, but now in an activist key, with the hopes of setting our work to work. Hopefully, the "we" being invoked here is affiliational and not presumptive. So too, the history being referenced is far from universal, but starts within the idea of the research university (even in the U.S. these number but a tiny fraction of all colleges and universities) in order to imagine what departures are possible from there. The first wave of interdisciplinarity we associate with the late nineteenth century creation of modern disciplines, with a corresponding architecture of departments and representation by professional associations. While the disciplines as we know them all have their creation myths, they are formed out of mixtures from other fields — philology and history for modern languages and literature, parsings of political economy and philosophy for sociology, etc. Interdisciplinary projects, like the invention of race drew from biology and statistics, sociology and philosophy, literature and visual arts, in ways that forged a sturdy bond between disciplinary and national boundary, between a unique technique of knowing or methodology, and a distinctive ethno-cultural belonging. Just as the models for higher education in the United States hybridized German and British national forms, the civic mission of the university promised to acculturate the national citizen through disciplinary knowledge. This national narrative was the idiom by which business and professional class interests could be expressed although certainly without exhausting what capital and labor could claim for the university.

The second wave of interdisciplinarity emerges with the massive state intervention in higher education from tuition subsidies like the G.I. Bill and the 1958 National Security Act and the public investments in campus construction. Development discourse that proclaimed convergence between recently liberated colonial states and the metropolitan centers who claimed to be all grown up offered a biological analogy to geopolitical dynamics. Follow in the parents' footsteps and you'll turn out just fine. This teleology was brokered by an epistemological exchange. Embrace systems models and analytic methods, and the other will achieve the status of a knowable object through the likes of area and ethnic studies. The heroes of this salvage operation will be the knowledge entrepreneurs — those who master a field, make it their own by coming to know all that can be known about it. In this, the PMC profession makes proprietary claims for restricted trade that set-up the deregulation of intellectual property for financial gain. While departmentalization is still the campus gold standard, interdisciplinary programs can thrive through external funding and what is too-often unselfconsciously referred to as empire building. The combination of knowledges, the value of external funding, the celebration of academics ability to be at the center of this whole-scale production is termed a revolution in a manner referencing not the Bolshevik, but the industrial form. While the professional associations are at the apex of their power when campus growth-driven demand puts a premium on expanded credentialization, so too are the great combines of industrial unionism, which reached a height of membership in the 1950s and peak militancy in the 1970s. While maintaining a craft identity, the ascendancy of the professional class across all manner of occupations constitutes a socialization of managerial labor and industrialization of the knowledge economy that drives a fulsome unionization of academic labor in the public sector.

In this third wave of interdisciplinarity, characterized by what has been called here the professional turn in the midst of a risk economy, the figure of the arbitrager emerges. Once again, neither professional specialization, nor the academic entrepreneur have gone away, any more than departments and interdisciplinary programs have fallen by the wayside. Instead they operate according to different logics. Added to the inventory of academic programs are the post-professional. In the most general terms this references the largest growth area for student enrollments increasingly captured by proprietary institutions like Phoenix University so that now 2,452 of the 6,412 colleges and universities are for-profit (and fewer than 150 institutions are considered research universities). The for-profit sector is absorbing students today the way the state institutions did forty years ago. Wage volatility and professional class decomposition mean that education becomes the medium for sustaining lateral (or downward) mobility in the labor force. It is the place where labor goes to retool after having gained a suddenly useless bounty of real-life experience. In the United States, over 100 million students are enrolled in these adult or continuing education programs which catalogue every conceivable teachable human activity and efface the boundary between work and leisure, professional self development and personal enrichment, career counseling and self-help. Closer to the bone of academic specialization are graduate degree programs that exist off the return or re-entry of professional labor into the academy. This is a sign of the decentering of the university in relation to industrial knowledge production but also of the circulation between knowledge production inside and outside the university.

The vast supermarket of educational opportunity is met by the niche of the post-professional program in a manner that sets the instructors of record in motion as arbitragers. Within the university they take these typically small programs to advertise the innovative worldliness of the institution, but also open any number of alliances between universities and other industrial sectors to which the moment of critical reflection and elaboration may matter greatly to the drift of industry. The post-professional program is specialization along the lines of a derivative. It is occasioned by a generalized volatility in the market that makes recombination of knowledges to hedge against specific imaginable risks. But this specialization marks a generalized condition, the prospect of speaking through expertise from any location that can have more generalizable effects. Artists, scholars of the middle east, students of american labor find themselves elevated — like the terrorist — from a concrete and delimited capacity to a well nigh universal potency of the sort associated with the voice of the state. The organizational cognate of this voice is the political party, the voicing of a generalized situation of political affairs. While the conventional political party is by measures of preference and loyalty in decline, the party function to generalize a politics from a particular platform now has the potential to spread.

So, these three waves of interdisciplinarity can now be thought not in some incessant temporal succession, but in more explicitly spatial and organizational terms. Together they allow for an amalgamation of the major organizational forms of the past century: the craft or professional association; the industrial union; and the political party. By means of a spirited commitment to administrative labor, these three organizational registers can (and do) get traversed in a manner that offers a new instantiation of interdisciplinarity itself. The professional association also refers to faculty and university governance, to the committee-work that affords the long-march through the institutions and to administrative posts that mediate and ameliorate certain demands of faculty — above all this is where new interdisciplinary entities come to life. The industrial form makes a virtue of the relation between the university's inside and outside, and transforms marketization from a passive or defensive pliant to a strategic intervention in the socialization of labor. Finally, the party-form — perhaps most alien to freedom loving academics who may not always notice how and when they speak to comprehensive issues of power that invoke the state — permits a set of claims to be launched that extend beyond any epistemological or institutional site. This triumvirate of affiliations is for some already in our midst. It treats the externalities of nation, class and market as media through which we already circulate and turns the poster children of capital into knights of labor. This is a tall order for interdisciplinarity, but one which makes all the difference in the world out of what is already to hand. It only requires a re-elaboration of the work we do along the way.

PART II

Hierarchies in the Market for Education

Lean and Very Mean:
Restructuring the University in South Africa
Franco Barchiesi

O n 24 February 2000, Professor Colin Bundy, Vice-Chancellor of the University of the Witwatersrand and esteemed intellectual of the left, "regretfully" announced that the University's Council had approved the retrenchment of 600 employees working in services such as cleaning, maintenance, catering and transport. The retrenchment was part of a plan of "fundamental changes" called Wits 2001. Wits 2001 was designed by a 5-person committee that includes Bundy, the deputy vice-chancellors and Wits' human resource manager. The plan seeks to reduce the number of faculties at the university from nine to six and to replace the current 99 departments with approximately 3040 "academic entities."

The Wits administration argues that restructuring is a necessary response to significant cuts in the tertiary education subsidy, declining student numbers, proliferating numbers of courses and collapsing morale among academic staff. The plan targets three areas: the number and size of academic entities, appropriate staffing levels, and staff-to-student ratios.

A new Academic Restructuring Review Committee (ARRC), appointed by the Council, is making the recommendations. Academic Planning and Restructuring Committees at the faculty level will propose measures to implement the restructuring plan. Faculties and executive deans have been given three years to adapt their priorities to the program outlined by the ARRC.

Their only real task, however, is to ensure that scarce resources are used "cost-effectively." The power to define priorities and distribute resources remains highly concentrated in the university's "senior executive team." In other words, the restructuring process follows a typical pattern of technocratic decision-making that confines the debate to how to use the resources allocated from the top to comply with priorities also determined at the top. Staff, students and workers were offered no meaningful input into the decision-making process.

The administration's assessment of Wit's situation deliberately avoids to consider important expenditures other than staffing and employment such as management-related remunerations, costly infrastructures such as "anti-crime" electronic security gates and image-related investments like vehicle access gateways. The administration has not accounted for the University's financial reserves and patterns of investment in exploring ways to cut costs. Since the administration has the power to exclude such data from the restructuring agenda, downsizing seemed to be the only logical option.

University as investment

The reorientation of the state has given rise to the "corporate university": a business enterprise able to sustain itself with market profits, a powerful economic actor in local economic restructuring, an institution thus able to attract staff, students and investment on a global scale. The notion of "academic excellence" thus can be measured across the global academic marketplace. Like business notions of "quality" and "professionalism," "academic excellence" becomes the yardstick against which global capital can measure its "opportunity costs" and profit potentials of investing in specific tertiary institutions.

These radical changes to South Africa's education policy have evolved in a context marked by spiralling unemployment and corporate restructuring, resulting in approximately 100,000 job losses a year in the first five years of ANC rule. New employment is usually casual or contract. Student enrolments at Wits have declined in this context from 19,396 to 17,735 between 1991 and 1998, after 20 years of steady increases in student registration.

It can be argued that the combination of the impoverishment among the waged population, rising unemployment, widening social inequalities and increasing employment insecurity is leading families to conclude that they cannot afford a university education for their children, especially when its "marketable skills" are already in question. These processes reflect similar forms of exclusion from other commodified social services such as health care, water, electricity and housing. It indicates the failure of the nascent South African democracy to define a model of university that is accessible to the demand for knowledge coming from marginalized communities.

The 1999 Shaping the Future strategic plan provided a broader intellectual agenda for restructuring at Wits. The plan states that: "In order to compete, universities have had to become most cost-conscious and less reliant upon tradition and externally funded autonomy," intensifying "the trend from 'collegial' to 'managerial' governance of universities." If the rise of the corporate university involves a new emphasis on the institution's capacity to reduce "externally funded autonomy," the consequence is that an increasing share of the university's income will depend on attracting private investment and redefining the university's own role as an investor.

Such changes are emphasized in Wits' Income Generation Programme (IGP). Shaping the Future defines one of Wits' priorities as research that is focused on target areas such as socioeconomic problems, health (i.e. cooperation with private hospitals), engineering, and technology. At the same time, a "University company" has been proposed for the "optimization of revenue opportunities from intellectual property and from entrepreneurial activities" and to "promote revenue-generating activities and create approaches for entrepreneurial approaches across the university." Wits' IGP is funded in part by 1 million rand provided by the mining corporation Goldfields. More money is being sought from Anglo/De Beers, the Ford Foundation and major financial conglomerates Investec, Coronation and Liberty Life. The program's former director, Robin Lee, describes the program as a step towards redefining Wits as an "enterprising university" or a "business university."

The idea behind the IGP is for staff to relinquish permanent, publicly-funded posts and become dependent on selling courses to wealthy private clients. The IGP seeks to "initiate and drive changes in the ways in which significant sectors of the university are funded and managed." These include outsourcing and subcontracting catering, residences, and, more ominously, research.

In short, the proposals to downsize and retrench are not just responding to contingent needs for "rationalization." Rather, they had already been conceived as necessary to foster Wits' economic efficiency in the eyes of investors and to boost the concept of the university-as-corporation. This also means that student recruitment and admissions will have to be run "entrepreneurially, rather than bureaucratically," casting serious doubt on democratizing access to tertiary education in South Africa.

University as investor

The IGP portrays a future in which the university itself becomes an investor in local economic restructuring, for example, by developing new technologies for the mining or telecommunications industries. The University of Manchester Institute for Science and Technology (UMIST), which administers all of that university's research through a wholly-owned, self-sustained private company, is an example for the IGP. The role of such a company is to regulate research contracts and to identify the private funders/customers. Such customers, in turn, ensure the "viability" and profitability of university research. In this model, the university becomes a franchising agency that allows its "brand" to be used only in projects that respond to the needs of economic actors that are powerful enough to guarantee an economic return. This is a far cry from the notion of the university as a public research institution promoting a diversified, general, and critical knowledge. Moreover, there is a danger that departments and faculties will be rated according to their "income generation" potential, which will greatly determine future decisions about restructuring and downsizing. The market thus becomes the central regulator of intellectual life while at the same time disciplining critical and dissident voices into providing research that meets market needs. Only in this way can university intellectuals avoid carrying the brunt of the next "rationalization" phase.

Since the vision implies an increasing delegation of funding arrangements and research outcomes to the private sector, this process can best be described as one of privatization even if Wits will remain a nominally public university. All that would be left of the intellectual context of the university would be a notion of "academic excellence" as a way to mobilize the loyalty of academics through emotional, consent-generating buzz words such as "world-class African university" at the service of the "Renaissance" and the "progressive" aim of breaking the domination by "bureaucracy." Left-wing academic support is thus recruited for a project that de facto redefines the main function of higher education as boosting corporate capital's profit-making capacity.

The events at Wits are the culmination of four years of intense restructuring that has affected all major South African tertiary institutions. A common thread, often disguised behind the moral imperative of equalizing the resources allocated to "historically black" and "historically white" institutions, has been a renewed emphasis on the market as a decisive regulator of intellectual life. The 1997 recommendations of the National Commission on Higher Education, for instance, endorsed new university structures geared towards public-funding policies that emphasize "applied" education, cost-effectiveness and partnership with external public and private actors.

The restructuring process has been accompanied by managerial rhetoric aimed at identifying the "market potential" and the income-generation capabilities of programmes, curricula, courses, research and publications. In a situation where increasingly, departments and "entities" will be run as independent business units, corporate investors and top academics teaching "marketable" courses in "marketable" faculties would be liberated from the burden of subsidizing programmes or departments that are not cost-effective. At a June 1999 workshop hosted by the Sociology Department at Wits, Deputy Vice-Chancellor Leila Patel said that in the future, departments will have to raise their own income, including by offering short courses for affluent private clients. This would mean the end of the "age of tenured employment," since the university would provide employment only to its internationally-renowned academics. The latter will be joined by casual or contract lecturers who will depend on marketing their courses for their income. In this way, Bundy has been able to spin his announcement of the creation of 20 junior lectureships (13 year contracts) for "previously disadvantaged" population groups as socially responsible.

Nothing sells like "excellence"

The end of apartheid led oppressed and exploited communities to increase their demand for tertiary education, modifying the composition of student bodies in previously segregated institutions. While in principle this has abolished the distinction between "historically black" and "historically white" institutions, in practice such a distinction remains. It is visible in many aspects of academic life, including staff composition (which at universities like Wits, Natal, UCT and Afrikaans-speaking institutions is still predominantly white), curricula, support programmes and entrance requirements. Black students remain overwhelmingly the target of academic exclusions due to outstanding debts and the inability to pay admission fees. According to the Department of Education, while black students will comprise 73 percent of all university enrolments in 2001, the number of students in need of financial aid also will double by 2010.

Given the rapid increase in the number of students in financial need, the annual increase in government funding for tertiary education between 1995 and 1998 of approximately 9 percent was in fact a decrease in real terms. Then Minister of Education Sibusiso Bhengu underscored the point: "higher education has to be paid by the recipients and not by the state."

As confirmed in the government's 1999 Budget Review, the emphasis on promoting "technological education and training" has meant that state subsidies for institutions with a stronger humanities and social science component have been slashed. The subsidy for Wits has declined by nearly one third in the past five years.

While enrolments at the 21 universities declined by 6 percent between 1997 and 1998, student numbers at the 15 "technikons," which are more oriented to techno-professional skills, rose by 20 percent over the same period. In 1988, 272,445 students enrolled at universities and 56,815 registered for technikons. Ten years later these figures were 351,692 and 250,244 respectively.

Fight back

Resistance at Wits, as elsewhere, has been led by the 100,000 strong National Education Health and Allied Workers' Union (NEHAWU) until now. NEHAWU is facing the loss of 600 members and plans industrial action in response to the retrenchments. The decisive challenge will be to build a united movement among all university constituencies.

Yet staff members are confused and divided. The progressive-sounding rhetoric of the restructuring is coupled with opportunities offered by the new corporate university to a minority of them. The university administration is able to present restructuring as inevitable. These processes have greatly moderated the opposition of this constituency. Student politics is also weakened by defeats suffered by previous movements, and movements have been contained through a variety of tactics that include student expulsions, criminal charges and police actions. As recent episodes such as the seven-month strike at Mexico City's Autonomous University (UNAM) and the occupations at John's Hopkins University have shown, the unity of all university constituencies is crucial to raise broader popular support for struggles against the marketization and privatization of public education.

Governmentality and Commodification: The Keys to Yanqui Academic Hierarchy

Toby Miller

Eighteenth-century European Enlightenment knowledges invented social collectives and liberal individuals. Since that time, populations have been understood through statistics and policy interventions — the social body assayed and treated for its insufficiencies. Governing people came to mean, most critically, combining science and government to maximize civic management and economic productivity. Such developments coincided with and cross-pollinated economic transformations that forged industrial and finance capitalism.

In this brief piece, I aim to explain how the history of US universities is characterized by an expansion of governmentality, in the sense of research undertaken for the public weal and teaching that reaches into the lives of the populace to train it in self-regulation; and an expansion of commodification, as research becomes animated more and more by corporate needs, students are increasingly addressed as consumers of education, and paymasters and administrators accrete authority over academics. Both tendencies increase hierarchization. Many writers working within the governmentality tradition do so in a way that assumes an incommensurability with Marxist critique. I see no logical reason for this. I acknowledge that the project of neoliberal governing-at-a-distance has its own logics and materialities; they fit the agenda and methods of corporatization as much as governmentality. I argue that both tendencies have been at play since the emergence of higher education as part of public culture in the US 150 years ago, but that neoliberalism has maximized their influence in recent times. The classic US model of higher education aims to equip students with a liberal inclination that respects knowledge of a topic and for a purpose, rather than simply knowledge by a particular person. The model places its faith in a discourse of professionalism rather than charisma. It urges people to believe in and exchange openly available knowledge, not secret magic. In other words, if someone truly wants to know how television works, she is permitted access to this intelligence. But she may equally subscribe to digital cable simply based on her confidence in the system of governmental and university research, industrial training, and accreditation that impels and regulates this fraction of a culture industry. She need not do so based on the idea of audiovisual communication as a gift from a deity to an elect whose knowledge and power cannot be attained by others. Of course, liberalism also uses the concept of human capital — that there should be a mutual investment of time, money, and training by both society and subject to create a corps of able-minded technical employees and willing patriots who are taught by a docile professoriate — the idea of higher education as an industry, and students as investors. Hence Bruce Johnstone, a former Chancellor of the State University of New York, offering the concept of *learning productivity* as part of students beginning to "assume greater personal responsibility for their learning." How did this state of affairs come to pass? Since the 1830s, when the first waves of white-settler European immigration across classes began, US higher education has generated practices and knowledges for use by the state and business and to integrate the population. By the 1850s, with the country rapidly industrializing, new chiefs of industry envisaged partnerships with tertiary education to develop a skilled workforce. Abraham Lincoln's Republican Party enabled this alliance via the land-grant system. Technocratic from the first, it flowered at the turn of the century, when corporations were placing more and more faith in applied science via electromagnetism, geology, chemistry, and electricity. By the 1920s, Harvard had its business school, New York University its Macy's-endorsed retail school, and Cornell its hotel school. No wonder, then, that Thorstein Veblen referred to US universities as "competitors for traffic in merchantable instruction." His words remain accurate in their diagnosis (even if their style looks old-fashioned). The two World Wars provided additional pump priming and premia on practicality from the Federal Government, and the big research schools actually expanded their capacity during the Depression. Today, a financial dependence on private sources is twinned with what we might call the mimetic managerial fallacy, a process whereby both governments and university administrators construct corporate life as their desired other. This not only makes for untimely influences on the direction of research and teaching, but on the very administration of universities, which are increasingly prone to puerile managerial warlockcraft superstitions about excellence and quality control.

Academic institutions have come to resemble the entities they now serve — colleges have been transformed into big businesses. Major research schools, particularly private ones, are also landlords, tax havens, and research-and-development surrogates, with administrators and fundraisers lauding it over Faculty. Decanal apparatchiks have essentially replaced Faculty governance. College bureaucrats are making a transition to full chief-executive-officer stature. The mimetic managerial fallacy also leads to more and more forms of surveillance from outside. Regional accrediting institutions vouching for the quality of US degrees have been in place for well over a century. But since the 1970s, we have seen ever-increasing performance-based evaluations of teaching conducted at the departmental and Decanal level, rather than in terms of the standard of an overall school. Today, such methods are used by 95% of departments. These systems directly link budgets to outcomes, in keeping with the prevailing beliefs of public-policy mandarins — their restless quest to conduct themselves like corporate elves manqués. As successive superstitions came along — the 1990s variety was Total Quality Management — administrators fell in line with these beguiling doxa. Along the way, Faculty-student ratios worsened, and reporting, surveillance, and administration grew in size and power.

Many of us who have actually worked for business and government know what laughably inefficient institutions they can be — but then, those who watch academics do research and teaching from the perch of administration frequently have ressentiment in their eyes and underachievement on their résumés. In the research domain, the notion of mutual interest licenses partnerships between state, college, and industry, dating back to 19th-century museums, observatories, and agricultural-experimentation outposts. The shop was really set up in the late 1950s. The Cold War stimulated growth, increasing federal and state subsidies. Considerable effort since then has gone into clarifying the significance of tailoring research priorities to governments and corporations. Consider linguistics (the scandal of language-spread policy); political science (Project Camelot in the 1960s); economics (Robert Triffin acting as plenipotentiary for the US to the European Economic Community and then as a European delegate to the International Monetary Fund, just a few months apart, in the 1980s); sociobiology (defenses of male sexual violence); and psychology (participating in torture during the latest War on Islam). The very existence of communication research raises questions of ideological distortion, given the discipline's formation under the sign of war and clandestine state activity and later corporate and foundation support. The same could be said of the policy sciences. Originally conceived as points of connection between democratic and executive action, they have degenerated into expertise that lacks articulation with everyday people, connoting pro-corporate/pro-Christian positions that turn highly contestable positions into absolutes, with consultant professors simultaneously performing objectivity and applicability. This history predates contemporary concerns about how to finance US research universities since the system lost relatively disinterested Cold War stimuli to big science in the early '90s.

Today, it appears as though governmentalization and commodification have merged in their concerns and methods. Congress provides more than a billion dollars in direct grants to universities, apart from the peer-reviewed funds available through the National Science Foundation and the National Institutes of Health. But whereas corporations gave US schools about $850 million in 1985, the figure was $4.25 billion a decade later. The NSF established dozens of engineering research centers in the 1980s with the expectation of "partnerships" flowering between corporations and higher education. Such centers have effectively functioned as ongoing public welfare for "entrepreneurs." Industrial research parks now dominate the work of such schools as Texas, Massachusetts, Duke, North Carolina, and Stanford. And MIT's media laboratory is a playpen provided by corporations for well-meaning but apolitical graduate students working with implicit and explicit theories of possessive individualism — an ethos of fun in which the latter may privately claim to be subverting their paymasters, but where they do so in ways that are eerily reminiscent of the dot-com boom's empty cybertarianism. The extraordinary Bayh-Dole Act of 1980 permits nonprofit educational institutions to own and commercialize inventions, provided that the state can use them as it sees fit. Prior to the Act, research schools collectively accounted for about 250 patents a year. Now the figure is close to 5000. Perhaps 3000 new companies have emerged as a consequence of the legislation.

It should come as no surprise that US universities are increasingly business-like entities, at times taking legal action against their own researchers to make as much money as possible. The idea of working in the public interest has been erased through amendments to state laws throughout the country that have quietly exempted publicly-funded scientists from conflict-of-interest responsibilities that apply to refuse workers and personnel officers. Medical drugs are a case in point. US deregulation has propelled marketing into the forefront of drug development, and pharmaceutical corporations (pharmacorps) deem old-school academic research and education too slow for their financial rhythms. Recent evidence suggests that marketing as much as medicine determines how to develop a new chemical compound once it has been uncovered: whether it will be announced as a counter to depression or ejaculation; whether it will be promoted in journal x or y; and which scholars will be chosen to front it and produce consensus about its benefits. Leading figures in medical schools and professional practice routinely accept monetary and travel gifts from companies as a quiet quid pro quo for favorable publicity of this kind. Pharmacorps budgets for marketing to clinicians have skyrocketed, and they pressure medical journals to print favorable research findings in return for lucrative advertising copy. Major advertising agencies that work with pharmaceutical companies, such as Interpublic, WPP, and Omnicom, have subsidiaries like Scirex that even conduct clinical trials. Known as medical education and communications companies, they brag about "getting closer to the test tube."

The desire for sales and speed versus the need to observe protocol meet, ironically, in scholarly journals, which the giant pharmaceutical multinational Pfizer describes — rather alarmingly — as a means "to support, directly or indirectly, the marketing of our product." Little wonder, then, that medical education and communications companies provide ghostwriting services, paid for by corporations, that deliver copy to academics and clinicians — and pay them for signing it. One in ten articles in the leading US medical outlets are today estimated to be the work of ghosts, and 90% of articles about pharmaceuticals published in the Journal of the American Medical Association derive from people paid by pharmacorps. Faculty are shilling for corporations by allowing their names to go on articles that they have neither researched nor written — for all the world like footballers or swimmers who have never even read, let alone penned, their "autobiographies." Instead, these corporate subsidiaries write the papers on behalf of academics. The prevalence of ghostwriting has led the International Committee of Medical Journal Editors to establish criteria that require authorship attribution to verify who undertakes the research and writing that go into manuscripts. It's good to see that editors of the leading medical journals are speaking out against these dubious practices. But next time you are perusing a CV that includes endless four-page articles signed by 27 people allegedly working together on pharmaceuticals in a laboratory, the field, or clinical trials, you might want to ask whether the real "author" was even listed. And you might begin to query the assumption that the sciences and medicine are at the heart of scholarly rigor. When Barthes wrote of the "death of the author," and Foucault described writers as "author functions," their ideas were belittled by many. But using such insights, perhaps it is time to name and shame the ghostly figures who produce so much "scholarly" literature, and expose the farcical faculty who function as the public face of this deceit — perched atop research schools. Turning away from research, we can see a tendency across the entire degree-granting sector of transferring the cost of running schools away from governments and towards students, who are regarded more and more as consumers who must manage their own lives, and invest in their own human capital.

In 1980–81, the three levels of government accounted for 48.3% of higher education funding, whereas the proportion was 38% in 1995–96. This trend towards reliance on tuition doubled student debt between 1992 and 2000. One thing is common across US higher education — the crisis of student debt in an era when tertiary studies are financed more and more at personal cost. For a decade and a half, tuition increases have outstripped inflation, rocketing beyond stagnant levels of federal aid to students. As a consequence, corporate lenders have become central to financing undergraduate degrees. Private debt has more than tripled in the last five years, to $17.3 billion in 2005–06. And while Federal loans are capped at a 6.8% interest rate, private ones can soar as high as credit-card levels — 20%. New legislation makes defaulting on such loans through bankruptcy virtually impossible. So even as students are increasingly being told — rightly — that only a college education can deliver a middle-class lifestyle, they are facing accumulated debts of $100,000. And that's before they enter professional schools to become lawyers or doctors, when they will need much bigger loans.

Shifting the burden onto students to be financially responsible for their education supposedly makes them keener learners, while encouraging additional scrutiny of the classroom is said to aid them in a space of traditionally unequal relations of power. But that Pollyannaish analysis will not do. First, as more and more funding in fact comes from private sources, it is they who are acting governmentally to ensure returns on their investments, both ideologically and monetarily. Second, addressing students as liberal agents both distorts their actual subject-positions, and under-prepares them for the obedience and absence of free speech required in most US workplaces, in addition to adding to the central power of has-been and never-were academic administrators over working scholars. And what of those working scholars? The world of hiring varies enormously, based on the class structures that divide academia. My department is currently searching for two jobs. They are not in the sciences, or in professional categories that carry salary loadings. The candidates won't be expecting, say, $200,000 as start-up funds with which to build their research in the expectation of large grants that will help pay for university administration. Nor will they expect to be remunerated as though they were suffering the slings and arrows of opportunity cost by not working in corporate America. I am speaking above of those privileged few who have tenure or tenure-track positions in Research-One schools. Most people teaching in universities are freeway professors who travel feverishly between teaching jobs, cobbling together a living, or folks working full time in second-tier schools with gigantic course loads. Inside the top universities, there is also great variety. When I was a full professor of cinema studies, American studies, and Latin American studies at NYU, I was paid four-fifths of the salary of the average starting untenured assistant professor in the law school, and one tenth of the salary of a particular advanced assistant professor in the medical school (she worked on fertility drugs, so this figure was not typical of her cohort). How did I know this? In the case of the law school, through senior people who told me. In the case of the medical school, even private institutions are obliged by Internal Revenue to disclose their top three salaries to public view. In general, divide-and-conquer is the leitmotif of these schools. However, the notion that one's income is a matter of privacy is a technique for preventing employees from sharing information and hence being able to lobby collectively. This is aided by the Supreme Court's Yeshiva decision, which holds that full-time faculty at private universities are managerial employees, and hence have no right to engage in collective bargaining, i.e. via a union. The wager that such schools make is that you won't demand what you don't know you can have. One thing's for sure, the negotiations for our current positions on offer won't be as complex as those involving a guy I knew who moved to an Ivy League school a few years ago and told me that his new department had to work overtime to guarantee his $500,000 a year personal travel budget. Nor will they equate to the person I used to work with whose deal promised her time and money for weekly visits to a different city to ensure continuity with her preferred therapist. And these discussions will differ from those entered into by thousands of adjuncts each year as they await last-minute phone calls and messages asking them to teach courses to hundreds of students, because full-time faculty are doing their "own" work. The discussions won't reference the experience of students looking for the "professor" who taught them last quarter, who didn't have an office, who won't be back this year—and is forgotten by all concerned other than the personnel office, which has closed her file until the call goes out again for the reserve army of the professoriat to emerge from freeway hell in time of need. And the future? Apart from the large number of undergraduate students and cultural-studies professors watching reality-TV shows, the idea of the makeover resonates monumentally with US colleges. Several high-profile schools have undergone huge transformations in recent times. The first instance was probably Duke University. Set up and supported by tobacco money and plantation history, the North Carolina campus spent vast sums of money from the 1980s in order to elevate itself into the top echelon of Research One universities, hiring people from all across the world to improve its standing. In the early 1990s, NYU decided to do the same thing. It embarked on a massive fundraising campaign amongst its trustees and others who were keen to make the scene as major benefactors in the Manhattan philanthropy set. Following Duke's model, NYU decided that it needed to improve its standing in the basics of a university — the arts and sciences. It already had highly-ranked law and medical schools, but they are professional entities as much as research centres and do not generate scholarly esteem in the same way that mathematics and history can do, for all the power they exercise in the university and the wider society. Studies indicated that a massive influx of renowned faculty into the arts and sciences could have an immense and immediate impact on the quality of graduate-student applications, and then on to undergraduates. In less than a decade, NYU went from a second-rate commuter school to having top-notch students from all 50 states and half the world. How were professors attracted to move? Huge salaries, New York City, buying whole departments to keep stars company, light or nonexistent teaching loads, generous travel money, spousal hires, and a sense of making a difference. What was this like for those who were already in place? The Law School didn't care — it had absolute independence financially and managerially, other than in the naming of a Dean. The Medical School was absorbed in its own version of a pressing national issue: what to with white elephants (AKA teaching hospitals). The low-rent professional schools, like Education and the Arts, were left out, because they didn't fit the paradigm, and exercised little or no power on campus other than as public symbols. People who had toiled away in lowly-ranked arts and science departments were variously flattered and angered by the sudden appearance of superstars and their baggage of psyches, somas, libidos, and lofts. The latest school to follow this model is the University of Southern California. Located in south-central Los Angeles, where the rebellion occurred after the Rodney King trial of 1992, USC has long been a bastion of wealthy, not-very-smart white students and faculty skirting an area of multicultural poverty. Again, it had excellent professional schools, and also boasted a renowned athletics department; but in the basic research areas — not so much. USC was widely regarded as standing for "University of Spoilt Children." No longer. Nowadays, schools that it has raided for top talent refer to USC as the "University of Stolen Colleagues." All the money that comes each time the football team wins is now being cycled into buying the best faculty across the basic disciplines. In New York, the challenge was to look good alongside other private schools, notably the nearest Ivy League representatives, Columbia and Princeton. In California, the point of comparison is public schools, notably the University of California system's leading lights, UCLA and Berkeley. It will be a while before USC can compete seriously with those testaments to the wisdom of public-cultural investment. But it will get there. If there is a lesson here, it is that the coarseness of commuter campuses and homely professors can be made beautiful. Money remaketh the university. Neoliberal "reformers" in other countries are fond of referring to the decentralized, mixed-market model of US colleges as a beacon. The truth is that this model's success relies on long-established, disinterested ruling-class wealth, in the case of the Ivy League, and competitive boosterism by individual States, in the case of the public sector. When the actual costs of running universities are passed on to students, the results can be devastating. And the crisis contributes to a wider national problem of gigantic personal indebtedness. It does so in the context of governmentality and commodification — today's recipes for academic hierarchy, Yanqui-style.

The Social Production of Hierarchy and What We Can Do About It: Notes from Asia

Xiang Biao

Institutionalized education in most of human society seems intrinsically hierarchical. One is supposed to progress from a "lower" level of learning to the "higher"; "average" kids study in mediocre schools, and the "outstanding" go to top colleges; and finally, "degree" is by definition hierarchical. Recent discussions on higher education have focused on the governmentalization/corporatization (roughly meaning tightened administrative management in order to make universities managerially accountable) and the marketization of universities. This essay explores the logic of hierarchy making in a larger, societal context. It is beyond dispute that established institutions have a deeply vested interest in maintaining exclusive and hierarchical systems, and it is also true that hierarchy, particularly in the form of the ranking tally, is imposed top down by the establishment. However, we should not deny that educational hierarchy is also widely recognized, respected and sometimes even celebrated by larger society. Nor should we reduce public acceptance to merely an example of false consciousness. Most people know much better than us (university nerds) how to deal with the world. There are ethnical and moral dimensions to the socially produced hierarchy. Instead of aiming to eradicate hierarchy altogether (which cannot be a feasible agenda despite the ideological appeal), this essay wishes to explore the social process of hierarchy-making which may enable realistic action agendas.

Precarious Hierarchy and the Ethnics of Hierarchy

In modern times, higher education became less exclusive, and educational hierarchy became much less absolute. In colonial Asia, for example, formal English education had such a magic power that it directly contributed to the creation of the institution of modern dowry in India. It is also safe to say that, in Asia at least, higher education became less hierarchical in the so-called neoliberal era. (I use neoliberal era with some reluctance. By this term I am referring to the period starting at the end of 1970s for China, the beginning of 1990s for India, the early 1990s for Japan, and the late 1990s for South Korea.) China launched a new, unprecedented round of university expansion in 1998. The number of newly admitted students jumped from 1.08 million in 1998 to 2.5 million in 2001. By 2007, the planed intake reached 5.67 million! Similar to Japan and South Korea, entering universities is no longer a crucial life event — it is not difficult to get in, and furthermore getting in does not guarantee good job prospects. Students have more freedom in choosing universities according to location, subject or campus "culture" instead of a single system of hierarchical evaluation.

But hierarchy certainly does not go away. Universities have become ever more concerned about hierarchical ranking. Shanghai Jiaotong University produces one of the best known tallies in the world. This reflects the fact that previously fixed hierarchy is replaced by more dynamic and unstable differentiation. Hierarchy is in struggle. This also suggests that the process of hierarchy making becomes more public, or social, than before when it was declared by the state or established by tradition.

Underlying the new project of hierarchy making in higher education is a unmistakable capitalist logic. The higher rank a university secures, the higher tuition fees it charges. But the opposite is untrue. In general, students cannot enter a high-rank university simply by paying more fees. There is a limit to capitalism. A curious example is the mushrooming MBA courses in China. On the one hand, no other institutions are more conscious than the MBA programs about hierarchical ranking, which directly determine the fees they charge. On the other hand, most of the MBA students, particularly those enrolled in the elite institutes in China, have work experience and many are self employed, thus the ranking does not mean much for them in the material sense (say, compared to other students who may need a strong university brand for looking for jobs). When I asked an entrepreneur (incidentally, a Taiwanese) why he applied for an expensive MBA course in Shanghai, he gave me three reasons: good teachers, the reputation of the course ("it sounds good"), and the opportunity to prove that, after working for many years, he is still able to pass tough examinations. The Chinese capitalist class in the making need symbolic capital, but they need "solid" symbolic capital, i.e., not cheap counterfeits.

The hierarchical ranking of universities undoubtedly facilitates exchange between financial and cultural capital. But, simultaneously, while different types of capital are exchangeable, each capital must maintain minimum autonomy. Thus, in order to be acceptable to the general public, hierarchy must be based on "merit" to some extent. Universities also have to maintain a balance. For example, elite universities in the US charge high fees but also provide generous scholarships. Scholarships attract good students to keep rankings high which in turn justifies high fees.

In China. at least until very recently, socially produced hierarchy in higher education has significant moral connotations. For example, lecturers and students from top universities are expected to be more vocal in criticizing the status quo, and the state has to be more careful in dealing with professors from these institutions. In a largely authoritarian and politically conservative system, this status provides the institutions with special clout to be more independent, critical, daring in thinking alternatives, and sometimes more eccentric in behavior. People rank the universities high to counteract the state power and private economic interest, no matter how symbolically.

New Battles

Hierarchy itself may not be a problem. The issue is what kind of hierarchy prevails. Our goals should be, apart from continuing the historical progress of destabilizing and "softening" hierarchy in general, making the hegemonic hierarchy more ethical.

In Asia as well as elsewhere, states have been active in domesticating and incorporating the institutions that are high up in the hierarchy. The corporate world may have similar desires, although their efforts are less orchestrated and their relations to universities less clear. But, both the state and the economic establishment need seemingly independent universities for the purpose of legitimation. (Say, the state occasionally needs some "independent scholars" to back their views, and financial institutes also like donating money to "independent" learning institutes.) The contradictions internal to the project of legitimation provide important space for actions. Furthermore, the interests of the state and of capital do not always fit well, and playing one off against the other can be another strategy.

I cannot quite imagine autonomous universities in a practical sense. As Mao Zedong repeatedly reminded us, intellectuals are a piece of feather who cannot exist without someone else's skin. We need others for our material survival. But perhaps we can fight for a more "autonomous" evaluation system with strong moral and ethical concerns. Another important battle field is pre-university education. I am not too worried about the corporatization or privatization of universities as I believe that it will not go too far. Even state bureaucrats and diehard capitalists would frown upon universities that have no intellectual or ideological teeth at all. What is much more dangerous, for China, is the ongoing process of privatization and hierarchization in secondary education. As it is less easy for money to infiltrate into higher education, well-off families start the race early. Parents spend thousands of US dollars to send children to good primary and high schools and even kindergartens. (In Beijing, top kindergartens literally charge thousands of dollars for a seat.) In Japan, elite private universities such as Keio and Waseda set up their own so-called "escalator" system including kindergartens, primary and secondary schools. Children from wealthy families buy the expensive ticket to enter the escalator on the ground floor, which takes them to the top universities in the future with certain "merits." Thus social inequality is produced and reproduced without upsetting the merit-based hierarchy of universities. In China, except those who are desperate to consolidate their newly acquired financial assets into firm class status, most people want to escape from the frenzied competition in which children became the main victims. Thus there is a social base for mobilization to fight against this trend. Among other things, top universities may be able to do something, even symbolically, to counteract the education industry.

Border as Method, or,
The Multiplication of Labor

Sandro Mezzadra and Brett Neilson

The current globalization of university systems needs to be rethought in the wider context of changing forms of mobility, the production of geographies that project themselves across the limits of modern political spaces, and the forms of policing that emerge with the proliferation of borders within as well as beyond such limits. We have in mind not only the transnational mobility of students and academics but also the increasingly elaborate systems of higher education export, outsourcing and franchising that are emerging with the penetration of Anglophone universities into market contexts such as India and China. What interests us about this is not so much the emergence of education as a commodity subject to GATT and WTO rules of trade like any other, but rather how the intricate geography implied in the production of education as a global commodity involves the continual remaking and redrawing of the borders that classically separate universities from their outsides.

One aspect of this is the crisis of the "university of culture" so effectively described by Bill Readings over a decade ago. Yet the loss of the university's mission of safeguarding the national culture is not the only factor at play in this transition. It is also necessary to consider, in a transnational frame, how the value-form of knowledge is being repositioned not only with respect to labor market positions (of students, graduates, researchers, etc.) but also with regard to funding arrangements, knowledge transfers, intellectual property regimes, and so on. These changes imply a complexification of the filters and gatekeeping functions that control access to the university for students and other figures as the bearers of labor power. In the first round of Edu-factory discussion, this remaking of the borders of universities was referred to as a system of differential inclusion. This involves an elaborate system of assessment patronage, trade, language skills, visa issuance and border control that places universities in a transnational frame and produces and reproduces labor market hierarchies at different scales.

It is no accident that the concept of differential inclusion has also been used to describe the filtering of migrants at the borders of the EU, US, and other continental, subcontinental and national spaces. But to recognize that the processes and technologies of differential inclusion are also at work in the context of global higher education is by no means to draw a simple homology between say international students (or other university workers) and undocumented and/or other labor migrants. The situations of these subjects are clearly disparate, even if they can also overlap. Nonetheless, it is important to note and analyze the commonalities and diversities of these border-crossing practices and experiences to map the effects of the concurrent processes of explosion and implosion that characterize the interlinked and heterogenous geographies of labor extraction today.

In this essay we want to make two main points:

1. That it is insufficient to model these multifarious and interlinked systems of differential inclusion using the concepts of governmentality and the international division of labor.
2. That any possible escape from the commodified global university must also involve political practices of translation that question the dominance both of international English and/or national languages.

To turn to the first of these points, we can remember Toby Miller's valuable contribution, tracing the tendency for US universities to transfer costs away from governments and towards students, who are regarded more and more as consumers who must manage their own lives. Contrary to many other writers working in the governmentality tradition, Toby argues that this situation requires an analysis that mixes Foucauldian theories of liberal governance with Marxist critique. We couldn't agree more. But when we begin to map the ways in which the global expansion of US universities sets up patterns of subsidy and investment on the transnational scale, we need a new set of concepts and methods adequate to the analysis of the borderscapes that emerge.

We are less interested in a critique of governmentality that finds its impetus in the current forms of exception than one that explores governmental techniques and modalities of rule in their normative moments. The concept of governmentality can only account for the infinite repetition of nuanced variations on the same theme of a given model of liberal subjectivity. Furthermore, despite the dispersal of governmental mechanisms across the prismatic geography of global/local dynamics, there are moments of excess implied in the continuous production and reproduction of the unitary and coherent conditions that make the workings of the technological and legal mechanisms of governmentality possible. Consider the establishment of US universities, in which liberal education and English language instruction are practiced, within specially designated zones in China (for a strictly delimited period of time). The deployment of zoning technologies is a crucial character of development in post-reform China (one needs only to think of special economic zones as the one established in Shenzhen): whatever the practices within these higher education institutions, zoning technologies cannot be reduced to the logic of governmentality. Rather their deployment points to the intertwining of governmentality and sovereignty as a necessary feature of the emerging transnational production system in higher education.

In this case, the borders between the university and its outsides obtain a complexity that cannot be fully explained by the concept of the international division of labor or the correlate spectrum of skilled, semi-skilled and unskilled workers. What we face is a situation where labor continually multiplies and divides with the global proliferation of borders, in this instance the internal borders of China. Multiplication, we should emphasize, implies division, or, even more strongly, it is a form of division. But, when it comes to the globalization of university systems, division works in a fundamentally different way than it does in the world as constructed within the frame of the international division of labor. It tends to function through a continuous multiplication of control devices that correspond to the multiplication of labor regimes and the subjectivities implied by them within each single space constructed as separate within models of the international division of labor.

Corollary to this, and relevant not only to the current globalization processes in the university sector, is the presence of particular kinds of labor regimes across different global and local spaces. This leads to a situation where the division of labor must be considered within a multiplicity of overlapping sites that are themselves internally heterogeneous. To put it simply, to make sense of the characteristics of the contemporary global geography of production and exploitation, one has to consider at once a process of explosion of previous geographies and a process of implosion by which previously separated actors are forced into interlinked systems of labor extraction. While this intensifies modes of exploitation, it also leads to a multiplication of lines of flight and possibilities for new forms of transnational social and political cooperation and organization. While capital divides labor in order to produce value added, the multiplication of labor provides opportunities for new practices of subtraction or engaged withdrawal.

This leads us to the question of auto-education and autonomous university experiences that emerged in the first round of Edu-factory discussion. In "Colonial Difference," Jon Solomon expressed what we think is a very legitimate worry: that the various attempts to construct alternative or nomadic university experiences might end up reproducing ossified forms of national and cultural resistance to the neoliberalization of the university. This is a real danger and we would be lying if we were to claim that we have not ourselves experienced situations where it is precisely this that threatens to occur. But we would also like to emphasize that this is not necessarily so. Indeed, an attention to what we have above been calling the multiplication of labor implies a practice of subtraction that must necessarily involve practices of translation that work against the retreat to national culture in the face of global English and the consequent inattention to the seemingly contradictory complicity of nationalism and neoliberalism.

The practice of translation we have in mind demands a new political anthropology of organization and a rethinking of the very notion of the institution which is a far cry from the trite calls for universal languages and transparent forms of discourse that have occurred on this list. What these polemics fail to recognize is that any practice of translation that attempts to flatten all meanings and affects onto a single plane of arbitration will imply incommensurabilities and miscarriages in communication, even if the conversation is occurring in a national language. We couldn't agree more with the Counter-Cartographies Collective when they write about the tendency for critical intellectual and activist idioms to divide and separate. But we do not see this tendency as one that can or should be remedied by the imposition of a single mode of address that would close the differences at play. The task is rather to work in and through translation and to join this work to a politics that recognizes that capital itself attempts to close such heterogeneity by abstracting all values onto a single plane of equivalence.

By rethinking translation outside the frame of equivalence and neutral arbitration between languages, it is possible to distinguish patterns of multiplication and proliferation of meaning that do not result in a politically dehabilitating dispersion of forces and alliances. Conversely, such a heterolingual approach to translation does not imply the reduction of political thought and action within a series of haphazard articulations that are nonetheless constrained by the existing institutional arrangements. To reconceive the political within this frame is not to obscure or abandon its conflictual dimension. The practice and experience of struggle is not incommensurable with a practice of translation that does not seek to level all languages onto an even field. Such translation, however, does lead us to ask how a politics of struggle in which one either wins or loses can be thought across a politics of translation in which one usually gains and loses something at the same time.

Since translation is a practice, we find it more useful to speak of it in practical rather than theoretical terms. For us, translation is never simply about language — it is a political concept which acquires its meaning within plural practices of constructing the common. On the other hand, it implies conflictual processes and struggles that constellate about the heterogeneity of global space and time. To return to our initial concern about borders and border-crossers, we might mention the work of the Frassanito Network. Founded after a border camp protest in Puglia, where a number of internees managed to escape from an illegal detention center, this network links a number of groups across Europe and beyond doing political work around movements and struggles of migration. Neither simply an autonomous university nor a group of activists, the practice of translation is fundamental to the modes of organization instituted by this network. We can mention, for instance, the transnational newsletter *Crossing Borders* (http://www.noborder.org/crossing_borders/), which has been published in up to ten languages.

At stake here is not simply the communication of a stable message to readers in different language groups but the entry of translation as a practice of political organization that is central to the constitution of the network. The production of these texts across languages necessitates a time and space of organization that is fundamentally different to that which would emerge in the absence of this practice. This is only one instance in which translation becomes a principle of political organization that constitutes new forms of struggle and movement that reach toward the global scale and question the division of activist from migrant that has plagued many political efforts in this regard. We do not want to celebrate this mode of organization or to claim it is without its problems. Nor do we want to forward it as a model for other attempts to invent new institutional forms. Political invention, to be short, cannot be cut and pasted. What we can state is that organizational forms that seek to move beyond the dyad student-citizen, which continues to animate many attempts to oppose the corporatization of the university, will have to involve translational practices that exceed the conceptual and political frame of governmentality.

The Pedagogy of Debt

Jeffrey Williams

S tudent loans, for more than half those attending college, are the new paradigm of college funding. Consequently, student debt is, or will soon be, the
new paradigm of early to middle adult life. Gone are the days when the state
university was as cheap as a laptop and was considered a right, like secondary education. Now higher education is, like most social services, a largely privatized
venture, and loans are the chief way that a majority of individuals pay for it.

Over the past decade, there has been an avalanche of criticism of the "corporatization" of the university. Most of it focuses on the impact of corporate
protocols on research, the reconfiguration of the relative power of administration and faculty, and the transformation of academic into casual labor, but little of it has addressed student debt. Because more than half the students
attending university receive, along with their bachelor's degree, a sizable loan
payment book, we need to deal with student debt.

The average undergraduate student loan debt in 2002 was $18,900. It
more than doubled from 1992, when it was $9,200. Added to this is credit
card debt, which averaged $3,000 in 2002, boosting the average total debt to
about $22,000. One can reasonably expect, given still accelerating costs, that
it is over $30,000 now. Bear in mind that this does not include other private
loans or the debt that parents take on to send their children to college. (Neither does it account for "post-baccalaureate loans," which more than doubled
in seven years, from $18,572 in 1992–1993 to $38,428 in 1999–2000, and
have likely doubled again).

Federal student loans are a relatively new invention. The Guaranteed Student Loan (GSL) program only began in 1965, a branch of Lyndon B. John-
son's Great Society programs intended to provide supplemental aid to students

who otherwise could not attend college or would have to work excessively while in school. In its first dozen years, the amounts borrowed were relatively small, in large part because a college education was comparatively inexpensive, especially at public universities. From 1965 to 1978, the program was a modest one, issuing about $12 billion in total, or less than one billion dollars a year. By the early 1990s, the program grew immodestly, jumping to $15 billion to $20 billion a year, and now it is over $50 billion a year, accounting for 59 percent majority of higher educational aid that the federal government provides, surpassing all grants and scholarships.

The reason that debt has increased so much and so quickly is because tuition and fees have increased, at roughly three times the rate of inflation. Tuition and fees have gone up from an average of $924 in 1976, when I first went to college, to $6,067 in 2002. The average encompasses all institutions, from community colleges to Ivies. At private universities, the average jumped from $3,051 to $22,686. In 1976, the tuition and fees at Ivies were about $4,000; now they are near $33,000. The more salient figure of tuition, fees, room, and board (though not including other expenses, such as books or travel to and from home) has gone up from an average of $2,275 in 1976, $3,101 in 1980, $6,562 in 1990, to $12,111 in 2002. At the same rate, gasoline would now be about $6 a gallon and movies $30.

This increase has put a disproportionate burden on students and their families — hence loans. The median household income for a family of four was about $24,300 in 1980, $41,400 in 1990, and $54,200 in 2000. In addition to the debt that students take on, there are few statistics on how much parents pay and how they pay it. It has become common for parents to finance college through home equity loans and home refinancing. Although it is difficult to measure these costs separately, paying for college no doubt forms part of the accelerating indebtedness of average American families.

Students used to say, "I'm working my way through college." Now it would be impossible to do that unless you have superhuman powers. According to one set of statistics, during the 1960s, a student could work fifteen hours a week at minimum wage during the school term and forty in the summer and pay his or her public university education; at an Ivy or similar private school, the figure would have been about twenty hours a week during term. Now, one would have to work fifty-two hours a week all year long; at an Ivy League college, you would have to work 136 hours a week all year. Thus the need for loans as a supplement, even if a student is working and parents have saved.

The reason tuition has increased so precipitously is more complicated. Sometimes politicians blame it on the inefficiency of academe, but most universities, especially state universities, have undergone retrenchment if not austerity measures for the past twenty years. Tuition has increased in large part because there is significantly less federal funding to states for education, and the states fund a far smaller percentage of tuition costs. In 1980, states funded nearly half of tuition costs; by 2000, they contributed only 32 percent. Universities have turned to a number of alternative sources to replace the lost funds, such as "technology transfers" and other "partnerships" with business and seemingly endless campaigns for donations; but the steadiest way, one replenished each fall like the harvest, is through tuition.

Although state legislators might flatter themselves on their belt-tightening, this is a shell game that slides the cost elsewhere — from the public tax roll to individual students and their parents. This represents a shift in the idea of higher education from a public entitlement to a private service. The post-World War II idea, forged by people like James Bryant Conant, the president of Harvard and a major policy maker, held that the university should be a meritocratic institution, not just to provide opportunity to its students but to take advantage of the best and the brightest to build America. To that end, the designers of the postwar university kept tuitions low, opening the gates to record numbers of students, particularly from classes previously excluded. I have called this "the welfare state university" because it instantiated the policies and ethos of the postwar, liberal welfare state.

Now the paradigm for university funding is no longer a public entitlement primarily offset by the state but a privatized service: citizens have to pay a substantial portion of their own way. I call this the "post-welfare state university" because it carries out the policies and ethos of the neoconservative dismantling of the welfare state, from the "Reagan Revolution" through the Clinton "reform" up to the present draining of social services. The principle is that citizens should pay more directly for public services, and public services should be administered less through the state and more through private enterprise. The state's role is not to provide an alternative realm apart from the market, but to grease the wheels of the market, subsidizing citizens to participate in it and businesses to provide social services. Loans carry out the logic of the post-welfare state because they reconfigure college funding not as an entitlement or grant but as self-payment (as with welfare, fostering "personal responsibility"), and not as a state service but a privatized service, administered by megabanks such as Citibank, as well as Sallie Mae and Nellie Mae, the critical federal nonprofit lenders, although they have recently become independent forprofits. The state encourages participation in the market of higher education by subsidizing interest, like a start-up business loan, but eschews dependence, as it leaves the principal to each citizen. You have to pull yourself up by your own bootstraps.

This also represents a shift in the idea of higher education from a social to an individual good. In the postwar years, higher education was conceived as a massive national mobilization, in part as a carryover from the war ethos, in part as a legacy of the New Deal, and in part as a response to the cold war. It adopted a modified socialism, like a vaccine assimilating a weaker strain of communism in order to immunize against it. Although there was a liberal belief in the sanctity of the individual, the unifying aim was the social good: to produce the engineers, scientists, and even humanists who would strengthen the country. Now higher education is conceived almost entirely as a good for individuals: to get a better job and higher lifetime earnings. Those who attend university are construed as atomized individuals making a personal choice in the marketplace of education to maximize their economic potential. This is presumably a good for the social whole, all the atoms adding up to a more prosperous economy, but it is based on the conception of society as a market driven by individual competition rather than social cooperation, and it defines the social good as that which fosters a profitable market. Loans are a personal investment in one's market potential rather than a public investment in one's social potential. Like a business, each individual is a store of human capital, and higher education provides value added.

This represents another shift in the idea of higher education, from youthful exemption to market conscription, which is also a shift in our vision of the future and particularly in the hopes we share for our young. The traditional idea of education is based on social hope, providing an exemption from work and expense for the younger members of society so that they can explore their interests, develop their talents, and receive useful training, as well as become versed in citizenship — all this in the belief that society will benefit in the future. Society pays it forward. This obviously applies to elementary and secondary education (although given the voucher movement, it is no longer assured there, either), and it was extended to the university, particularly in the industrial era. The reasoning melds citizenship ideals and utilitarian purpose. The classical idea of the American university propounded by Thomas Jefferson holds that democratic participation requires education in democratic principles, so it is an obligation of a democracy to provide that education. (The argument relates to the concept of franchise: just as you should not have to pay a poll tax to vote, you should not have to pay to become a properly educated citizen capable of participating in democracy.) The utilitarian idea, propounded by Charles Eliot Norton in the late nineteenth century and James Conant in the mid-twentieth, holds that society should provide the advanced training necessary in an industrially and technologically sophisticated world. The welfare state university promulgated both ideal and utilitarian goals, providing inexpensive tuition and generous aid while undergoing a massive expansion of the academy. It offered its exemption not to abet the leisure of a new aristocracy (Conant's aim was to dislodge the entrenched aristocracy of Harvard); it presupposed the long-term social benefit of such an exemption, and indeed the G.I. Bill earned a return of seven to one for every dollar invested, a rate that would make any stockbroker turn green. It also aimed to create a strong civic culture. The new funding paradigm, by contrast, views the young not as a special group to be exempted or protected from the market but as fair game in the market. It extracts more work — like workfare instead of welfare — from students, both in the hours they clock while in school as well as in the deferred work entailed by their loans. Debt puts a sizable tariff on social hope.

Loans to provide emergency or supplemental aid are not necessarily a bad arrangement. But as a major and mandatory source of current funding (most colleges, in their financial aid calculations, stipulate a sizable portion in loans), they are excessive if not draconian. Moreover, as currently instituted, they are more an entitlement for bankers than for students. The way they work for students is that the federal government pays the interest while the student is enrolled in college and for a short grace period after graduation, providing a modest "start-up" subsidy, as with a business loan, but no aid toward the actual principal or "investment." For lenders, the federal government insures the loans. In other words, banks bear no risk; federal loan programs provide a safety net for banks, not for students. Even by the standards of the most doctrinaire market believer, this is bad capitalism. The premise of money lending and investment, say for a home mortgage, is that interest is assessed and earned in proportion to risk. As a result of these policies, the banks have profited stunningly. Sallie Mae, the largest lender, returned the phenomenal profit rate of 37 percent in 2004. Something is wrong with this picture.

There is no similar safety net for students. Even if a person is in bankruptcy and absolved of all credit card and other loans, the one debt that cannot be forgone is student loans. This has created what the journalists David Lipsky and Alexander Abrams have called a generation of "indentured students." We will not know the full effects of this system for at least twenty years, although one can reasonably predict it will not have the salutary effects that the GI Bill had. Or, simply, students from less privileged classes will not go to college. According to current statistics, the bottom quarter of the wealthiest class of students is more likely to go to college than the top quarter of the least wealthy students. Opportunity for higher education is not equal.

Debt is not just a mode of financing but a mode of pedagogy. We tend to think of it as a necessary evil attached to higher education but extraneous to the aims of higher education. What if we were to see it as central to people's actual experience of college. What do we teach students when we usher them into the post-welfare state university?

There are a host of standard, if sometimes contradictory, rationales for higher education. On the more idealistic end of the spectrum, the traditional ra-

tionale is that we give students a broad grounding in humanistic knowledge —
in the Arnoldian credo, "the best that has been known and thought." A corollary is that they explore liberally across the band of disciplines (hence "liberal
education" in a nonpolitical sense). A related rationale is that the university is
a place where students can conduct self-exploration; although this sometimes
seems to abet the "me culture" or "culture of narcissism" as opposed to the
more stern idea of accumulating knowledge, it actually has its roots in
Socrates's dictum to know oneself, and in many ways it was Cardinal John
Henry Newman's primary aim in *The Idea of a University.* These rationales
hold the university apart from the normal transactions of the world.

In the middle of the spectrum, another traditional rationale holds that
higher education promotes a national culture; we teach the profundity of American or, more generally, Western, culture. A more progressive rationale might
reject the nationalism of that aim and posit instead that higher education should
teach a more expansive and inclusive world culture but still maintains the principle of liberal learning. Both rationales maintain an idealistic strain — edu-
cating citizens — but see the university as attached to the world rather than as
a refuge from it. At the most worldly end of the spectrum, a common rationale holds that higher education provides professional skills and training. Although this utilitarian purpose opposes Newman's classic idea, it shares the
fundamental premise that higher education exists to provide students with an
exemption from the world of work and a head start before entering adult life.
Almost every college and university in the United States announces these goals
in its mission statement, stitching together idealistic, civic, and utilitarian purposes in a sometimes clashing but conjoined quilt.

The lessons of debt diverge from these traditional rationales. First, debt
teaches that higher education is a consumer service. It is a pay-as-you-go trans-
action, like any other consumer enterprise, subject to the business franchises
attached to education. All the entities making up the present university multi-
plex reinforce this lesson, from the Starbucks kiosk in the library and the
Burger King counter in the dining hall, to the Barnes & Noble bookstore and
the pseudo-Golds Gym rec center — as well as the banking kiosk (with the
easy access Web page) so that they can pay for it all. We might tell them the
foremost purpose of higher education is self-searching or liberal learning, but
their experience tells them differently.

Second, debt teaches career choices. It teaches that it would be a poor
choice to wait on tables while writing a novel or become an elementary school
teacher at $24,000 or join the Peace Corps. It rules out cultural industries such
as publishing or theater or art galleries that pay notoriously little or nonprofits like community radio or a women's shelter. The more rational choice is to
work for a big corporation or go to law school. Nellie Mae, one of the major

lenders, discounted the effect of loans on such choices, reporting that "Only 17 percent of borrowers said student loans had a significant impact on their career plans." It concluded, "The effect of student loans on career plans remains small." This is a dubious conclusion, as 17 percent on any statistical survey is not negligible. The survey is flawed because it assessed students' responses at graduation, before they actually had to get jobs and pay the loans, or simply when they saw things optimistically. Finally, it is fundamentally skewed because it assumes that students decide on career plans tabula rasa. Most likely, many students have already recognized the situation they face and adapted their career plans accordingly. The best evidence for this is the warp in majors toward business. Many bemoan the fact that the liberal arts have faded as undergraduate majors, while business majors have nearly tripled, from about 8 percent before the Second World War to 22 percent now. This is not because students no longer care about poetry or philosophy. Rather, they have learned the lesson of the world in front of them and chosen according to its, and their, constraints.

Third, debt teaches a worldview. Following up on the way that advertising indoctrinates children into the market, as Juliet Schor shows in *Born to Buy*, student loans directly conscript college students. Debt teaches that the primary ordering principle of the world is the capitalist market, and that the market is natural, inevitable, and implacable. There is no realm of human life anterior to the market; ideas, knowledge, and even sex (which is a significant part of the social education of college students) simply form sub-markets. Debt teaches that democracy is a market; freedom is the ability to make choices from all the shelves. And the market is a good: it promotes better products through competition rather than aimless leisure; and it is fair because, like a casino, the rules are clear, and anyone — black, green, or white — can lay down chips. It is unfortunate if you don't have many chips to lay down, but the house will spot you some, and having chips is a matter of the luck of the social draw. There is a certain impermeability to the idea of the market: you can fault social arrangements, but whom do you fault for luck?

Fourth, debt teaches civic lessons. It teaches that the state's role is to augment commerce, abetting consuming, which spurs producing; its role is not to interfere with the market, except to catalyze it. Debt teaches that the social contract is an obligation to the institutions of capital, which in turn give you all of the products on the shelves. It also teaches the relation of public and private. Each citizen is a private subscriber to public services and should pay his or her own way; social entitlements such as welfare promote laziness rather than the proper competitive spirit. Debt is the civic version of tough love.

Fifth, debt teaches the worth of a person. Worth is measured not according to a humanistic conception of character, cultivation of intellect and taste,

ledge of the liberal arts, but according to one's financial potential. Ed-
___ provides value-added to the individual so serviced, in a simple equation: you are how much you can make, minus how much you owe. Debt
teaches that the disparities of wealth are an issue of the individual, rather than
society; debt is your free choice.

Last, debt teaches a specific sensibility. It inculcates what Barbara Ehren-
reich calls "the fear of falling," which she defines as the quintessential attitude of members of the professional middle class who attain their standing
through educational credentials rather than wealth. It inducts students into the
realm of stress, worry, and pressure, reinforced with each monthly payment
for the next fifteen years.

Management's Control Panel

Marc Bousquet

Management's Dashboard: William Massy's "Virtual U"

> "Who among us hasn't longed to be in charge for just one day? Oh, the things we would change! Virtual U gives you that chance — the chance to be a university president and run the show." — William Massy, *Virtual U* "Strategy Guide"

William Massy's *Virtual U* is a "computer simulation of university management in game form" (Sawyer 28). Designed by a former Stanford vice president with a $1 million grant from the Sloan Foundation, the game models the range of powers, attitudes, and commitments of university administration.

In short, it provides a window into one of the more widespread versions of administrative consciousness and worldview — the ideal administrator in the world of "resource allocation theory," "cybernetic leadership," and "revenue center management." The use of such simulations, models, and games is widespread in bureaucratic, professional, service, and manufacturing training environments.

The "serious gaming" trend has seen the emergence of games designed to promote environmental awareness, armed forces recruitment, white supremacy, religious tolerance, better eating habits, approaches to living with chronic diseases, and so on: wherever there is real-world rhetorical and practical purpose, institutions and activist organizations have commissioned games to propagandize, train, inform and recruit. Both the U.S.

armed forces and Hezbollah recruit through downloadable PC-based games. Even public budgeting has resulted in an at least two gaming simulations designed to influence voters by shaping attitudes toward spending, in New York City and the Massachusetts state legislature.

Massy's game is a budgeting simulation. It draws upon two prominent strains of thought in contemporary university management, the "cybernetic systems" model of university leadership developed by Robert Birnbaum and resource allocation theory, specifically the principles of Revenue Center Management (RCM), of which Massy is a leading proponent.

It is also signally influenced by the Hong Kong design team selected by Massy and the Sloan Foundation, Hong Kong's Trevor Chan. Massy and the Sloan Foundation specifically selected Chan for his prior success with the PC game *Capitalism* ("The Ultimate Strategy Game of Money, Power, and Wealth," reviewed by PC Gamer as "good enough to make a convert out of Karl Marx himself"). Massy and Sloane felt Chan's game represented a "good match" with their "similar" vision of management strategy, and the code underlying Chan's *Capitalism 2* serves as the base for many of the modules in Massy's game.

There is only one viewpoint possible in Massy's *Virtual U.* Players can choose to be the president of several different kinds of institutions, but presidency is the only possible relationship to the campus.

One cannot choose to play Massy's budget game as a student, faculty member, taxpayer, employer, parent, alumnus, or nonacademic staff. The reasons for this design decision are abundantly clear and profoundly ideological. To the audience Massy addresses, only administrators are "decision makers." Only the presidency offers a viewpoint from which to "view the whole institution." As a result, every other standpoint in the game has reality only insofar as it represents a "challenge" to presidential leadership.

Faculty, students, staff, and all other constituents are treated in the game as "inputs" to the managerial perspective. The players have the power to "adjust the mix" of tenure-track and nontenurable faculty, as part of their overall powers to "allocate resources as they see fit."

The ease with which nontenurable faculty can be dismissed is accurately modeled. Storing hundreds of faculty "performance profiles," the simulation permits university presidents to troll through the records — including photographs — of faculty in all ranks in every department. As in real life, presidents may terminate the employment of the nontenurable with a keystroke — advancing a great variety of their presidential policy goals with relative ease.

What is actually being taught here? Players have to fire adjunct faculty while looking at their photographs. One thing that's being taught is the exercise of power in the face of sentiment: players quickly learn that you can't make an omelette without breaking eggs.

By contrast, the tenured faculty are represented as a much more difficult "leadership challenge." They cannot be easily dismissed — so many leadership priorities could be swiftly reached if only all of the funds tied up in tenurable faculty were released! But the tenured have to be offered expensive retirement packages to free money for other "strategic purposes." And as in so many other ways, the faculty tend to act irrationally in response to retirement incentives.

While the tenured faculty may represent a headache for the player-president, they do not represent any real opposition in the world of the game. There are no unions. In fact, as bored game players frequently reported, the game is almost impossible for the player-president to "lose," because no one else has any meaningful power.

This is particularly significant because it successfully models the virtually unchallengeable legal-political-financial-cultural supremacy underwriting contemporary management domination (in the U.S. model). The only question is: How much victory can one administrator stomach over ten years?

Admittedly, Massy's ambition is to train a leadership cadre in the habits of benevolence. Underlying the game's approach to the relationship of administrators to faculty is Robert Birnbaum's "cybernetic systems" model, which synthesizes much of the new organization and management theory of the 1980s into a moderately more faculty-friendly form.

Birnbaum amounts to a "left wing" of the university management discourse. The extent to which this is a "left" wing is highly relative. On the one hand, Birnbaum genuinely feels that education required a different kind of organizational management than business corporations.

Within limits, he defends the sometimes anarchic and unpredictable nature of "loosely coupled" academic organizations, through which administrative subunits retain conflicting missions and identities at least partially independent of organizational mission. Birnbaum correctly notes that the corporate wing of the leadership discourse decries his moderately more faculty-friendly posture as "as a slick way to describe waste, inefficiency, or indecisive leadership and as a convenient rationale for the crawling pace of organizational change."

Recalling the current popular trope for faculty managers of "herding cats," he sums up his own view of "effective leadership" by quoting Clark Kerr's ambition to keep the institution's "lawlessness within reasonable bounds."

The book with which Birnbaum launched his retirement was an effort to debunk three decades of "management fads" in higher education, including TQM (discussed in Chapter Two), and Massy's own RCM.

On the other hand, Birnbaum, together with many in his discipline, is the author of an approving portrait of management's strategic deployment of faculty committees and faculty institutions as the "garbage cans" of governance. Drawing on a trope circulated by Cohen and March and enthusiastically adopted by the leadership discourse a decade earlier, Birnbaum notes the utility to "leadership" of establishing "permanent structural garbage cans such as the academic senate."

He observes that task forces, committees and other receptacles of faculty garbage are "highly visible, they confer status on those participating, and they are instrumentally unimportant to the institution." Their real function is to "act like buffers or 'energy sinks' that absorb problems, solutions, and participants like a sponge and prevent them from sloshing around and disturbing arenas in which people wish to act."

As in Massy's model, for Birnbaum the term "people" ultimately means administrative "decisionmakers." "People" should keep the faculty garbage "away from decision arenas." Serving as co-editor of the ASHE reader on organization and governance in higher education throughout the 1990s, Birnbaum's views on the "cybernetics of academic organization" were widely influential, at least among those who were committed to models of university governance as leadership by strong management qua benevolent indulgence of one's "followers."

Essentially the cybernetic model is about managing feedback loops in an awareness of systematic interconnectedness. Viewing management as a "social exchange," Birnbaum emphasizes the extent to which management enters a preexisting environment "in which there are many 'givens' that restrict to a great extent what can be done," and that while it is possible for a president to transform a "Neil Simon comedy… into Shakespeare," it requires incrementalism and the willingness to provide others with at least the sense of agency, so that, as Birnbaum cynically notes, "in future years, they can reminisce about how they transformed themselves."

He concludes that leaders have to listen to the organizational environment — or more accurately, monitor it — and cannot simply command: "leaders are as dependent on followers as followers are on leaders," and "presidents should encourage dissensus."

This promotion of dissent is not to encourage organizational democracy. It's to provide more accurate information to "decision arenas" and reduce "leader error" in the larger service of more effectively inducing changes in the behavior and value of organization members.

At its core, the cybernetic management model isn't about enabling speech per se on the part of non-leadership constituencies, it's about harvesting information. While faculty or student speech can be a source of information, speech isn't the only or even the primary mode through which presidential "data are collected." (Hence the "assessment movement" sweeping administrations across the country.)

By contrast, Birnbaum often models the administrator as a speaker, often a very creative one, the author, director, or impresario of organizational saga and myth, with the power to "interpret organizational meaning." Rather than "inducing the alienation that may arise from giving orders," presidents should "try to get people to pay attention to matters of interest to the administrator."

This isn't about faculty democracy; it's about the usefulness to administrations wishing to create "organizational change" of a sense of democracy. Where propaganda and the creation of organizational myth or mission fails, leadership can always induce "organizational learning" with funding. Over time, units that fulfill institutional mission receive funding increases; units that don't, decreases. "[T]he subunit 'learns' through trial and error in a process akin to natural selection."

Both Massy and the Sloane Foundation are explicit in their intention to promote a managerial model of systems theory in *Virtual U.* As in Birnbaum's vision, the arc of the game is fundamentally incremental. Player-presidents get results slowly over time by tinkering with the environment in which other constituencies act, rewarding certain behaviors and punishing others, primarily with funding: "many of the decisions don't produce explicit reactions, but instead initiate trends and behaviors that evolve toward a desired result by the manager."

If Birnbaum might be called an "organizational Darwinist," Massy is a managerial Malthus. In his essay, "Lessons From Health Care," Massy praises the system of managed care for insurers' capacity to intervene in the doctor-patient relationship. Because an insurer's "denial of payment triggers organizational learning," hospitals, clinics, and practices "will be less likely to perform the procedure again in similar circumstances."

The same principle, of feeding those who collaborate with management's vision of "institutional mission," and starving out the opposition, governs every dimension of Massy's management training game. The game's organizing concept is the representation over a ten-year period of the consequences of presidential adjustments in annual budgeting.

As Massy's collaborator at the Sloan Foundation has it, "money" is the "yarn" that knits this vision together: "Every decision translates, directly or indirectly, into revenue or expense. In considering how to convey the university as a system, we concluded that there was no better way than the annual budgeting process. The way the player, or the president, finally sees the whole institution synoptically is through financial flows." Primarily employed in education schools (Columbia, NYU, U Kansas, etc.) as a teaching aid in graduate classes in educational leadership, the game's scenarios are generally introduced with a version of the driving fiscal imperative: "Your task… is to maintain steady revenue, at minimum, and preferably grow revenue and spend it in ways that advance the institution."

The game is meant to bring forth a particular administrative subjectivity. One dimension of the administrative personality it successfully evokes is information overload. The managerial desktop is full of data. But each datum represents a competing claim on resources. These resources can be translated into livelihoods and potential good deeds, or as Massy has it, "the diversity of values that abounds within any higher education institution." The overall effect is of fatigue, including moral fatigue: "Each group argues for its view in terms of high principles, often reinforced by the fact that success also furthers self-interest."

The reduction of reality to revenue flows becomes a solution for the chief feelings of the administrative standpoint, information overload and something that might be called "value fatigue." As one USC administrator quipped to David Kirp, "if you don't have a vision, RCM becomes your vision." The game teaches a very specific set of feelings and values to potential future administrators. It teaches the utility of maintaining a large disposable faculty both for meeting financial targets and for quick restructuring to meet new presidential priorities. It teaches what I call a "management theory of agency," in which managerial decisions appear to drive history.

It even teaches what can be called a "management theory of value," in which the labor of "decision makers" (a la George W. Bush, "I'm the decider!"), and not the strenuous efforts of a vast workforce, appears to be responsible for the accumulation of private and public good in the university labor process. As one community college president using the game puts it to his students at Columbia University: "Senior administrators are the engines that push an institution forward — and like a big train, the larger the institution the more engines must be strung together to drive the institution forward." (Hankin)

In the down-is-up world of education administration, it becomes possible for a group NYU students playing Massy's game to conclude that the game's "Improve Teaching" scenario would be best served by a massive acceleration in the hiring of adjunct lecturers.

Ultimately, the game teaches these future administrators the pedagogy that Paul Lauter sees is already immanent in the institutions that it models:

> Universities teach by what they are. When a great university with an $11 billion endowment helps impoverish an already indigent city by using outsourcing to push down dining hall wages, it teaches who counts, and who decides in today's urban world. When a great university stiffs its retirees at $7450 a year while setting up its CEO for a $42,000 a month pension, it teaches who is important and who is not. When the American city in which a great university carries out its medical research has a higher infant mortality rate than Costa Rica, lessons about priorities are being delivered. When 60–

70% of the teaching hours at a great university — and at many not at all great universities — are carried out by a transient faculty, many of them paid below the poverty line and provided with no benefits, offices, or job security, a redefinition of teaching as a "service industry" is being implemented.

There are really two distinct worlds of faculty experience being modeled in *Virtual U.* There is the world of the tenured faculty who must be more ponderously influenced, involving a fairly strenuous effort by administrators.

Relatively speaking, it takes a lot of administrator sweat and frustration to surmount the obstacles represented by the tenured — who ultimately must be provided their retirement incentives to get out of the way, and require the constant creation of new forums/garbage receptacles for their opinions. Subject to the Malthusian financial discipline and organizational mythmaking of the leadership cadre, as extensively theorized by Birnbaum, Massy and others, the world of the tenure stream is certainly no picnic for most faculty occupying it.

The world that the game models for the "other" faculty, our non-tenurable majority, is rather different. These folks can be dismissed quickly and cleanly. Despite representing the majority of the faculty, they require a minimal fraction of management time and attention. The extensive use of them permits game players to advance most dimensions of the institutional mission with greater speed.

And in this dimension of the game-play, the premium on management's capacity to swiftly "adjust the mix" of labor to its own changing sense of "mission," is where we find Massy and the Sloane Foundation's vision of the future.

At a University of Pennsylvania meeting full of administrators, game engineers and potential users of the game, Sloane project director Jesse Ausubel described his own background in modeling systems used for real-time command and control of complex energy-industry operations (such as an oil refinery). Somewhat wistfully, he observed that the current release of *Virtual U* is for "teaching and learning, not real-time operational control."

However, he continued: "It would not surprise if some of the people in this meeting help advance the state of the art in university simulation, so that in 10 years, we have models that serve for control, for decisive management. For the present, and it is a huge step forward, we have a game."

In the future, the Sloane Foundation promises us, all labor will act informationally, in the interests of real-time control by a yet more decisive management. There'll be no more noodling around with even the trappings of faculty democracy.

PART III

Cognitive Labor:
Conflicts and Translations

Report from the Greek Student Movement, 2006/2007

Dionisis

The university is an important factor in the regulation of youth mobility in Greece, as elsewhere. Young people that dream of a good life, or a career, study hard during high school, in order to get into university. From there, they wish for a degree, and a job.

During the last decade, things have been gradually changing. The rise of unemployment has struck a heavy blow on the young, as they have seen their dream vanishing into a black cloud of uncertainty.

Public university education in Greece declined heavily over the last decade. Less and less money is spent for building and equipment. University teachers face wage cuts, and temps replace full-time faculty, creating big problems in many schools. At the same time, the university and its professors are becoming more and more attached to the corporations and the market. The university needs resources in order to survive, resources that only rich companies are willing to provide...for a price.

So the market university is a reality in Greece, and so is the precarity of students' lives and futures. In this situation, a wave of neoliberal reforms came to push the university even more towards the direction of the market. After all, the university is one of the last refuges for the youth, a place to discuss, spend free time creatively, and study, away from the tense rhythms of high school or the labor market.

At the end of May 2006, the education minister announced the coming of a new law for the universities. The law included many minor and major changes. Most of them are quite close to the Bologna convention, but also some Greek originalities. Measures and deadlines would be introduced to kick students that failed exams out of university. The universities adopted an evaluation method dictated by the government, and made development plans according to corporate mandates. New school rules would be introduced; in general, things would be tougher on students and schools. The number of free books for students would be reduced. No promises of funding or agreement to any other demands of the students and professors would be given. Furthermore, the university campus would be made more accessible for police entry, a taboo in Greece since the fall of the coup in 1974.

This announced reform, in combination with the tough situation for students, set forth a chain reaction of university occupations all around the country, such as had not been encountered for decades. In a couple of weeks, almost all schools were occupied by students. Thousands of students took action for the first time. The schools were full of life, events were organized, and the demonstrations were huge, numbering tens of thousands all over the country.

It was a grassroots movement, since many of these people had never dealt with politics before in their lives, and yet they did everything they could to give life to school occupations and demos. Of course many student groups of all kinds (left, leftist, social democrat, autonomist and anarchist) were involved. But they couldn't manipulate it. For example, the Stalinist student party, that is controlled by the Greek Communist Party which is pretty big in Greece was left out because they didn't support the occupations.

The energy was amazing. At first, the government spoke about manipulated minorities, but the numbers were so big that they couldn't deny there is a problem.

After a couple of weeks of occupations, at the Athens demo of the 8th of June 2006, police hit the students with heavy repression. Many were injured and a few arrested. The excuse was the heavy rioting that usually takes place during these demos, coming from small or bigger groups of people. The provocation was answered with even bigger demos from the students, and more occupations. Soon, almost no department was open. The government retreated, promising that they wouldn't pass the law during summer.

Then things became calm in the universities for a couple of months. In September, exams took place normally, and the students failed to support the heavy strikes of primary school teachers demanding for better wages and more money for schools, that lasted for two months. The strike ended in a failure.

The scenery changed again in January, when the constitutional reform procedure began. The Right government, with the consent of the social democrat opposition, agreed on the need for reforms in educations, and promised to change Article 16 of the constitution, which forbids the creation of universities by private entrepreneurs. Only the state is free to found a university.

Then, after only a few days, the students revolted again. It was surprising how fast and massive the new wave of occupations was. Almost 350 schools were occupied. (In June it was 420, 93% of the schools in Greece.) Major demonstrations were held. They were not as alive as in June, but they were equally large and even more politicized. The students were more experienced now. They discussed more and found better ways of organizing. Also, throughout the last months, many new grassroots groups had been created and new people had joined in. They were more prepared this time. They asked for better funding and more independence for universities.

Then, something unbelievable happened. The main social democratic opposition party withdrew from the constitution reform procedure. They found some silly excuse and said that they would no longer take part in the whole process, which included also other kinds of reforms. (Their support is necessary for a constitutional reform.) The student movement had created a big crisis inside the party and within the whole political scene. Everyone was talking about the students' issue, about the situation in higher education, although not always in a good way.

But the government, despite their failure, didn't withdraw. They accused the social democrats of hesitating and announced that they would pass the infamous reform law for the university. The situation was bad for them, and that had to end.

The new reform law was even worse than the former one, including, as punishments for the occupations, a reduction in university funding through the introduction of a high maximum limit of teaching weeks. (If less than 13 teaching weeks are accomplished, the semester would be lost.) The occupations were actually considered as a threat to the university. The asylum was now meant to protect only the right of work and study, not the freedom of expression and political action.

Everyone was very angry. But they were also tired. It had been a month of occupations, and many had gone home. But they had to keep it up. So the struggle continued.

Many were really frustrated with the situation. The schools were closed, and every week there were demos all over Greece, often with heavy rioting. Greek society was polarized. The situation was very tense. Many asked for the arrest of the rioters. The policed responded, months after the 8th of June demo: on the 8th of March, the day that the new law was passed, a demonstration of 35,000 in Athens was struck heavily by police brutality. Hundreds were injured and 61 arrested, some with heavy charges. Of course the police hit the student blocks, and not the individual rioters.

Everybody was furious with the heavy repression. Big demos were organized, especially in Athens, and all other kinds of actions. But the students and the people were tired. The propaganda had done its work. The students were left alone and diminished, and the reform law was passed.

At the moment of this writing, 23rd of March, the occupations still go on in about 200 schools, but they are decreasing. Probably by Easter Vacation, they will have vanished. Students are worried about semesters and exams, the reform is now law, and everything seems to return to normal. But the problems of the university are still here, as well as unemployment and precarity. No one knows what will happen in the future. No one is satisfied with the situation. And what of the dissenting students? Will they rise again? ...only time will tell...

Practices of Radical Cartography

Counter-Cartographies Collective

We write from a university in the American South which has contributed over an extended period of time to important progressive tendencies in the state and region, while at the same time struggling with its location in the antebellum South (slavery, low-wage extractive and assembly industries, segregation and civil rights, anti-communism, anti-unionism, and more recently strange interweavings of traditional conservatism, neoconservativism, neoliberalism, and populism). A state that reelected Jesse Helms as its Senator for over 31 years, recently launched a Presidential candidate who has explicitly called for universal health care and politics that is more directly attentive to the needs of the disadvantaged. These conflicted politics have sustained the university's own vision of its birthright and responsibility to the people of the state, and mean that — at least for now — the administrative structures of the university are not monolithic, but work as a complex meshwork of negotiated goals and interests. At the heart of this meshwork are students, faculty, administrators, alumni, staff, state and local politicians, business, and citizens of the state. Thus, the university continues longstanding traditions of faculty governance, engaged scholarship, and support for student activism and progressive community causes as it further embeds itself in the policy institutions of state and federal government as it draws on defense funding, as it links ever more closely to corporate funding streams, as it supports community development groups and schools at home and abroad, as it continues to be one of the few remaining loci of protected free speech in an emerging security state, as it... as a point of interest, UNC-Chapel Hill is the first public university in the country, many of its buildings historically constructed by African slaves, and has become today one of the most renowned universities in the US.

The Counter Cartographies Collective was born in this ambiguous yet exciting context. Different concerns, interests, anxieties and politics began to merge into a series of conversations in hallways and cafes. In particular a group of us were consistently gnawing at how to rethink forms of political intervention in the context of our campus and the US university more generally. The initial success and rapid failure of organizing drives such as the union that brought together both TAs and cleaners among other activist efforts left us organizationally disarmed. At the same time we saw the urgency of overcoming the language and affective vibe of the "ivory tower" which had many more pervasive effects than we had thought both within and without the university. How could we overcome both the anti-intellectualism amongst some political activists and the anti-activism of some critical intellectuals? We gathered different materials for inspiration in our search, material such as: The map of Bowling Green State University by subRosa cyberfeminists (http://www.cyberfeminism.net/biopower/bp_map.html), the impressive work of UT-Watch (at the University of Texas, http://www.utwatch.org/), and texts such as the exchange between Tizziana Terranova and Marc Bousquet in *MUTE* ('Recomposing the University," http://www.metamute.org/en/html2pdf/view/7148).

Our first collective steps can be traced to fall 2005. We put together an initial research intervention on the main campus when the administration cancelled the holiday on Labor Day, but only for certain employees — such as professors, teacher assistants, librarians, etc. — and gave the day off to the other sectors of its workforce. This blatant/insulting equation between knowledge work as non-work gave some of us the perfect excuse to raise the question of labor as a public and open target of discussion through the research dispositive of the drift, a stationary drift in this case (see "Labor Day Drift," http://countercartographies.org/index.php?option=com_docman&task=doc_details&gid=6&Itemid=32). Other interventions and presentation followed culminating in a long-term involvement to trace the multiple contours of the territory we inhabited and find ways of reinhabiting it.

Building on those experiences, our own desire to map our own territory, and the influence of contemporary activist research and radical mapping projects, especially Precarias a la Deriva and Bureau d'Etudes (see "Drifting Through the Knowledge Machine," in Biddle, Graeber and Shukaitis, 2007) inquiring into the multiple cartographies that compose our university. Following the long-standing tradition of the disorientation guides among campus activism in the US, we wanted one that was more graphical than the text-based production so far.

In the *disOrientation Guide* (http://countercartographies.org/index.php?option=com_content&task=view&id=15&Itemid=31) the Counter-Cartographies Collective tried to situate the modern research university as a complex scalar actor working at many different geographical scales. Located at the apex of the Research Triangle Park, one of the largest science research parks in the USA, the university and its sisters in the region, form a complex meshwork of knowledge institutions, the structure and consequences of which are currently in flux.

The map we produced sought to read the university in terms of three linked eco-epistemological frameworks: as a factory, a functioning body, and as a producer of worlds. These three points of our conceptual triangle each had their primary locus in the interest theories of Marx, the biopolitical and governmentality regimes of Foucault, and schizoanalysis and flat ontologies of Deleuze and Guattari. One of our main points was to render the university as a complex economic and political actor which, through its pedagogy, research, and other investments shapes particular regional worlds and promotes certain types of class divisions and diverse (at times precarious) modes of existence. In addition, the disOrientation Guide served/serves to arm its users with new tools, contacts and concepts to reinhabit, intervene in or subvert the university and its territories — a Re-Orienting function if you will.

In the summer of this year the 3Cs started tracing the development of Carolina North, a 250-acre industry/university collaborative research park that the University of North Carolina at Chapel Hill hoped to build on a large tract of forest a few miles north of the university. When we started our research, it seemed to us (and almost everyone else) that development on the new campus was inevitable and unchangeable: yet another example of hegemonic corporatization of the university.

As we talked to boosters and opponents, however, it became clear that even within the administration the vision of a new research campus was many things to many people. Some administrators argued that they needed top-of-the-line research labs with space for corporate offices in order to hire and retain top faculty, others framed that need more directly in terms of competition within the hierarchy of top-tier US schools to become a "world-class university." At other times and in other places the campus was cast as an economic development initiative for the State of North Carolina, a model of sustainable design, or even (just) a critically needed fix to shortages of research space on the main campus. Regardless of what they wanted, most everyone was already convinced that building a new campus would get it for them. Somehow, the one name of "Carolina North" managed to hold together a multitude of distinct and sometimes contradictory visions, and sediment them in space (or on paper, at least).

What follows is our attempt to catalogue the visions, logics and motives which produced the necessity and inevitability of a new university-corporate research park at our university. In some senses, then, this is a contextually specific project. However, many of the distinct logics we studied here in this place were explicitly global and national. Many of them are already part of the discussions on this list serve: hierarchization, corporatization, metrics (in fact, many of the items brought up in Toby Miller's contribution referring to the *mimetic fallacy* and new measures/bench marking of university performance are directly relevant to the project we're engaging in currently). Just as "Carolina North" articulated distinct logics together with contextual specifics, we contend that a set of broader logics and discourses is traveling the United States, and perhaps the globe, held together in the name of "the 21st Century University," "the global university," or "the world-class university."

This is not (just) the 3 c's of corporatization, commodification, and enclosure of the intellectual commons. Rather, we see a set of distinct forces, each with its own logics and discourses, which at this particular moment have coincided to form an apparently coherent vision for the future of the university. It is precisely because of its complex and contradictory nature that this vision is so powerful — it has become many things to many people. But this complexity also opens up new lines of flight. A cartography of the complex assemblage of "the global University" is our ultimate project.

We feel a need to trace the contours and topographical forms of our "university-in-flux" even to be able to begin to discuss what exactly this (or any) university is. To understand the "under-construction" composition of the university in order to discover what are our points of intervention: Is it a form to be resisted, defended against? Is it to be re-appropriated, hacked? In what ways is it a threat and/or an opportunity? Is it the end of one of the few bastions of critical thought in the Homeland Security state? Or can it become a form that can incubate more and more counter-institutions within and despite of itself (much like our own)?

Online Education, Contingent
Faculty and Open Source Unionism

Eileen Schell

Many American colleges and universities, like manufacturing and technology firms, regularly "outsource" jobs to save on labor costs and have been doing so for years: dining services, physical plant maintenance, parking services, and the list goes on. Outsourcing teaching is also a familiar phenomenon for many four-year colleges and universities. In "Outsource U: Globalization, Outsourcing, and the Implications for Contingent Academic Labor," John P. Lloyd argues that the "shift from the traditional tenure model of academic labor to the contingent academic labor model is itself a form of outsourcing."

Further, he cites an example of how the CSU system has explored "ways to outsource certain coursework to lower-paid contingent faculty at nearby community colleges." Although Lloyd reports on this strategy in 2004, I remember it as a common strategy twelve years ago when I was teaching at a southern university and the English Department there decided it no longer wanted to teach sections of basic or so-called "remedial" writing. The department simply stopped offering sections of basic writing and told students who had placed in the course to enroll in it a nearby community college. Many of the contingent faculty who would have taught that course ended up teaching it anyway at the local community colleges and for less pay. So outsourcing introductory or remedial courses to community colleges has been a way for four-year campuses to save money and to off-load the work they find too tedious or too expensive.

With universities and colleges increasingly assuming a business management model with an emphasis on labor flexibility and market responsiveness, it only makes sense that outsourcing will continue to increase. My goal here is explore the rise of outsourcing and online education and to discuss how open-source unionism can work to combat it.

The US has been a major incubator of for-profit universities. Perhaps best known of them all, the University of Phoenix models what these universities are all about — profit. Students meet in empty office buildings or rented spaces at night to attend classes or log-on to virtual campuses. Approximately 95% of all teachers at the University of Phoenix are contingent faculty working off the tenure-track: "While most colleges fight furiously over the top 25% of high school graduates, for-profits aim for the middle half of the class. They also target working adults hungry for technical and professional skills, including many lower-income ones. Even without affirmative action, almost half of for-profit students are minorities." (Symonds).

As Ana Marie Cox reports in her article "None of Your Business: The Rise of the University of Phoenix and For-Profit Education," in the past twenty years, "more than 500 new for-profit colleges and universities have opened their doors." Four-year for-profits have increased from 18 to 192, and 40 of those trade publicly on the stock exchange. "[One] quarter of the $750 billion spent each year on higher education stems from private, proprietary investment." University of Phoenix (owned by the Apollo Group) has earnings that surged 53%, to $247 million, as revenues jumped by a third, to $1.3 billion. Such stellar performance has given Apollo a market value of $11.4 billion — equal to the endowment of Yale University, the nation's second-wealthiest college" (Symonds, *Business Week*). The key question, though, is how has this impacted enrollments?

Ten of the biggest "publicly listed for-profits have already grabbed more than a half-million students. Add the hundreds of smaller players, and overall for-profit enrollment will jump by 6.2% this year, or five times the pace at conventional colleges, according to Boston market researcher Eduventures Inc. That will push the industry's revenues to $13 billion this year, up 65% since 1999" (Symonds). Higher education analysts "predict this segment will grow by about 20 percent a year, until it finally displaces nonprofit education."

For-profits also have grabbed 41% of the $3.5 billion online-degree market, which has tripled since 2000, according to Eduventures. They're aggressively expanding in foreign countries, too, targeting students in China, India, Chile, and other expanding educational markets. John G. Sperling, Phoenix founder and chairman of Apollo Group, predicts that as it rolls out online courses in developing nations, Phoenix could become the largest university in the world (Symonds). Let's be clear, though, distance education as a market is not confined to the private-for-profit sector. As David Noble points out in *Digital Diplomas*, most traditional colleges and universities have also developed online courses, setting up "for-profit subsidiaries" in the hopes of literally *keeping up with the Joneses* — like Jones International University (Noble).

For-profit educational institutions are profitable because they do not carry real estate and labor costs in the same way that traditional universities do. They make money because they don't keep up expensive grounds and expensive libraries and student centers — all things associated with traditional universities. They also do not make commitments to expensive, tenure-line faculty. They quite literally and quite nakedly make their money off of contingent faculty's backs. They "outsource" their entire faculty operation to contingent faculty or they employ a few big name professors to design online courses (course ware) that are then facilitated by online contingent faculty.

Yet if we are to read some of the latest portraits of contingent faculty in this brave new world of for-profit education, we are told that contingent faculty should become entrepreneurial in relation to such online environments and to the situation of contingency itself. Stemming from the managerial discourse so pervasive in US higher education, the adjunct as entrepreneur philosophy was pioneered by veteran contingent faculty member Jill Carroll, founder of AdjunctSolutions.com. Carroll has self-published two books: *How to Survive as an Adjunct Lecturer: An Entrepreneurial Strategy Manual* and *Machiavelli for Adjuncts: Six Lessons in Power for the Disempowered.* She is a veteran teacher of 12 courses per year at multiple institutions. According to Carroll, the key to becoming an adjunct entrepreneur is to develop courses like products: "Systemize their production until you can reap the benefits of economies of scale. Make them classes you can teach over and over, without mountains of preparation each time" (Smallwood). Her work publicized in the *Chronicle of Higher Education* in 2001 resulted in a regular column for a year in the "Career Network" section and spawned a number of spin-off articles about how contingent faculty are capitalizing on their contingency, especially in the online for-profit teaching market.

An April 30, 2004 *Chronicle of Higher Education* feature story intones that "for Online Adjuncts," it is a "Seller's Market." The article then proceeds to feature the life of contingent faculty entrepreneur Ruth Achterhof, a tristate online adjunct professor of business and management at four institutions: Baker College Online, Jones International, Davenport University, and the United Nations Development Program. Contingency is depicted as a blessing for Ms. Achterhof, a relief from the tedium of faculty meetings and the in fighting of petty academics. With a master's in educational leadership and a doctorate in organization and management, she tried the traditional classroom for a few years and was offered $35,000 a year to teach there permanently, which she turned down to take up online teaching in the late 1990s. She self-reports an income of $90,000 for juggling multiple online courses at a time, and her work days entail 14 hours a day in her computer chair typing email messages to students, responding to questions and posting work. Her work weeks taper off to four hours a day on Fridays and Saturdays, and Sunday is her sole day of rest. Despite this work week, she reports plenty of time to relax, including time to spend with her grandchildren. "I cook, I bake, I sew, I knit, I read...and I do sleep." She relishes the life, especially the idea that she'll never have to attend another faculty senate meeting, and imagines teaching online well into her 80s.

While Ms. Achterhof reports a large profit margin, others are less sanguine about the pay and benefits. As a University of Phoenix adjunct commented in a letter to the editor to *Adjunct Nation*, an online site, University of Phoenix's compensation package is hardly noteworthy: "Training is unpaid. The pay is usually $950 for a 5 week course with 13 students" with the expectation that the contingent faculty members are in "class" (read online) "at least 6 days per week." The estimated pay rate is usually "$6 to $10 per hour," although the college claims adjuncts make $50–80 per hour. As the adjunct writer puts it, "the tuition for undergraduate is $1,266 per 3-credit-hour course. Gross to University of Phoenix is therefore $16,454. Less $950 to me leaves a pre-other-expenses margin of $15,506 per course. In other words, the faculty member is paid only 5.7% of what University of Phoenix takes in for the class." This instructor reports that raises are not available until someone has taught there for 3 years, and that eligibility for the 401K matching dollars is not available to part-time faculty. The anonymous faculty member ends with saying he or she will take the training and find a more lucrative contract.

The online contingent faculty entrepreneur Ms. Achterhof and the anonymous unhappy contingent faculty provide opposite stories along the distance education continuum, and these are familiar stories of boon and bane. Yet the Carroll and Achterhof narratives are disturbing, as John Hess notes, because they offer a "trivialization of contingent academic labor and a dismissal of any collective approaches to changing its conditions" (Hess). Contingency is to be accepted, capitalized upon, and celebrated. This entrepreneurial rhetoric of the happy adjunct plays right into the entrepreneurial rhetoric of outsourcing and online education.

What should be done?

One hopeful arena for addressing change is through the international organizing of contingent faculty. The coalition-building efforts of the Coalition of Contingent Academic Labor (COCAL) has involved higher education contingent workers from the US, Canada, and Mexico, and the movement has been successful in building solidarity and resulting in increased visibility and gains for wages through local unionizing campaigns. These movements deploy what Richard B. Freeman and Joel Rogers refer to as "open source unionism," a way to describe unionization via Web technology. Like the open source software movement — "open source unionism embraces the utopian, collaborative ethos of the Internet revolution" (Schmid). As Julie Schmid notes in her excellent article "Open Source Unionism: New Workers, New Strategies," "[r]ather than depend on the traditional means of union organizing — leafleting at the plant gate, holding organizing meetings in the break from, or "house visiting" workers after hours...open source union organizing relief on cybertools such as listservs, chat rooms, and websites. These tools help bring together people who as a result of the new economy, are employed at separate locations, often as temporary or contract workers, and lack a common work experience." There is great potential here to organize workers across borders through open-source unionism, and there is also great potential here to organize students as compatriots in the struggle.

In my research into the outsourcing and contingency of faculty, I found evidence of many students joining in the struggle to organize contingent faculty and educate the general public about the working conditions of non-tenure-line faculty. If the collective voice of students can be joined with that of contingent faculty and with full-time faculty as well, we have a fighting chance. As Marc Bousquet argues, we need a"labor theory" of agency in higher education founded on a "rhetoric of solidarity, aimed at constituting, nurturing, and empowering collective action by persons in groups" ("Composition"). In contrast to a managerial theory of agency in higher education, which Bousquet defines as a emphasis on "institutionally-focused pragmatism," "acceptance of market logic," and "collaboration with a vocational and technical model of education," a labor theory of agency promises to open up spaces in higher education for worker solidarity and alliances across the lines of rank and position. A labor theory of agency in higher education is particularly urgent as the widely documented corporatization and globalization of higher education has accelerated the casualization of the higher education work-force. The now global struggle against casualization in higher education is about many things; it is about "job security and academic freedom and scholarly integrity and the public's trust in its institutional heritage," but in the words, of David Noble, "it is above all, about the preservation and extension of affordable, accessible, quality education for everyone who wants it."

Cognitive Capitalism and Models for the Regulation of Wage Relations: Lessons from the anti-CPE Movement

Carlo Vercellone

I. Cognitive capitalism, knowledge and flexibility

The mobilization of precarious young people and students which shook France in spring 2006 reflects contradictions related to the opening of a new historical phase of capitalism marked by the return in strength of the cognitive dimension of work and the constitution of a diffuse intellectuality. At stake is a change in the capital/labor relation that is directly opposite but comparable in importance to that which Gramsci, in the 1930s, anticipated in "Americanism and Fordism." It should be remembered that, during the postwar period, Fordist growth represented the result of the logic of development of industrial capitalism founded on three principal tendencies: the social polarization of knowledge, the separation of intellectual and manual work, and the process of incorporation of knowledge in fixed capital.

Following the crisis of Fordism, these tendencies were called into question and we actively experienced the rise of a new postindustrial configuration of capitalism: cognitive capitalism. By this concept, we refer to a system of accumulation in which the productive value of professional and scientific work becomes dominant and the central stakes in the valorization of capital relate directly to the control and transformation of knowledge into fictitious goods.

Contrary to the vision of an informational revolution, it is clear that the determining element of this transformation cannot be explained by a technological determinism which would make ICT (information and communication technologies) the principal factor of the passage to a new organization of the division of the labor and social relations. These theories forget an essential element: ICT can correctly function only thanks to a living knowledge that can mobilize them — because it is knowledge that controls data processing, information remains nothing but a sterile resource, like capital without labor.

Actually, the starting point for the formation of cognitive capitalism is the process of diffusion of knowledge generated by the development of mass schooling and the rise of the average level of education.

Knowledge is more and more collectively shared. It is this intellectual quality of the labor force which, breaking with industrial capitalism, led to the assertion of a new primacy of living knowledge, mobilized by workers, in contrast to the knowledge incorporated in fixed capital and the managerial organization of firms.

Two tendencies show the extent of this transformation of the social organization of work.

The first regards the dynamics by which the share of intangible capital (R&D, education, health), incorporated essentially in people, exceeded that of material capital held in stock and became the principal factor of growth. This change signals that the conditions for the formation and reproduction of the labor force are now directly productive. The principal source for the "wealth of nations" rests more and more on a productive cooperation located upstream from the organization of firms. It also follows that it is no longer possible to consider the constitution of the labor force (which is supposedly still in the process of being educated) through the old Fordist optic, which views the student as an inactive agent who carries out an unproductive activity undeserving of remuneration. This consideration is all the more relevant for another reason: the figure of the student and that of the paid worker, in particular of the poor worker, tend more and more to merge. Often this also has perverse effects with regard to the regulation of the labor market and the cumulative process of transmission and production of knowledge.

The second tendency relates to the passage, within a number of productive activities, from a Taylorist to a cognitive division of labor, where effectiveness rests on the knowledge and versatility of a labor force able to maximize the capacity of training, innovation and adaptation to a dynamics of continuous change.

In this context, one understands why, alongside the term knowledge, flexibility became the key word for characterizing the transformations to the regulation of the wage relation. The concept of flexibility, however, is extremely ambiguous and can move in two very different, if not contradictory directions.

On the one hand, it can refer to a policy that supports the training of the labor-force, taking into account increased education levels and privileging the competences of adaptability, mobility, creativity and reactivity to the unforeseen.

From a neoliberal point of view, on the other hand, it indicates the need for calling into question "rigidities" of the labor market which prevent wages and employment from adjusting themselves with fluctuations in economic activity. The term flexibility is here synonymous with a policy of generalized precarization of the labor force. This second type of flexibility is thus very different from the first. It can even have catastrophic effects on the mobilization of knowledge. The production of knowledge in fact requires a long term horizon and a safe income that allows workers to invest in continuous training.

Depending on whether priority is given to the first or the second sense of the term flexibility, there result two very different ways of regulating the wage relation in cognitive capitalism.

The first, which is Anglo-Saxon and neoliberal in character, also strongly inspired the development of the Lisbon Plan in Europe. It narrowly combines a hyper-technological and scientist design of the knowledge-based economy and economic policies directed towards the privatization of the commons and the rise of a rent economy. In this mode of regulation, the return on rent in its various forms (financial, real estate, patents etc.) has a place as much in the distribution of income as in methods for capturing the value created by work. It leads to an artificial segmentation of diffuse intellectuality and a dualistic configuration of the labor market.

In this configuration, a first sector concentrates an aristocracy of specialized intellectual work in the most profitable activities, which are also often parasitic on the knowledge economy. These include financial services for companies, research activities directed towards obtaining patents, legal counsels specialized in the defense of intellectual property rights, etc. This sector of the cognitariat (which one could also characterize as functionaries of capitalist rent) is well remunerated and has its competencies fully recognized. Its remuneration is integrated more and more into participation in the dividends of financial capital and the employees concerned benefit from forms of protection offered by the system of pension funds and private health insurance.

As for the second sector, it comprises a labor force whose qualifications are not recognized. The workers of this category thus end up undergoing a phenomenon of *déclassement* — i.e., a devalorization of their conditions of remuneration and employment compared to the competencies they actually put to work in their professional activities. This sector must not only provide the neo-Taylorist functions for the traditional sectors and the new standardized services, but also (and above all) occupy the most precarious jobs in the new cognitive division of labor.

The second mode of regulation corresponds to certain features of the Nordic and social democratic model, in particular the Swedish one. It acted as a way of associating a high level of social protection, a high general training level of the population, and the promotion of the collective dimension of a knowledge-based economy. However, in this model, because of the much more egalitarian character of income distribution and relations between the sexes, the structure of the labor market does not display the pronounced dualism of the Anglo-Saxon model. In particular, precarious jobs and the market for personal services have a less important role to play. The priority is given to the development of noncommercial collective services of high quality which constitute the driving sectors of the economy and provide employment in research and development. Let us note, however, that the cleavage between these two models of regulation, which has much to do with the typology of the social security systems established by Esping-Andersen, tends today to be exhausted. Everywhere in Europe, under the weight of financial pressures, we see a common tendency towards a process of "remarketization" of social security systems and the setting in place of so-called workfare policies.

II. France at the crossroads

In France, the constitution of a diffuse intellectuality and the genesis of cognitive capitalism were initially carried out under the impulse of conflicts which determined the crisis of the Fordism and allowed the development of a powerful welfare system. However, from the 1980s, the neoliberal inflection of economic policies led France to gradually adopt the Anglo-Saxon model of regulating the wage relation. Putting this model of regulation in place involved the multiplication of precarious forms of work (fixed term contract, interim, apprenticeship, subsidized employment, non-voluntary part-time labor, etc.) and a break from standard Fordist full-time and stable employment.

If the permanent full-time contract (DCI) still remains the standard for the majority of the French employees, the various forms of precarious and temporary contracts have grown to include 20% of all employment and more than 70% of new jobs. This process of precarization concentrated for the most part on two central categories of diffuse intellectuality: women and young people (most of them university graduates). In fact, precariousness as the norm of labor relations does not concern only manufacturing and less qualified employment. It is also very prevalent in the most intensive knowledge sectors, such as teaching and research, where the percentage of young precarious workers is among the highest. In addition, a growing number of young students or recent graduates are compelled to carry out training courses unpaid or with ridiculously low pay, while the work they perform is very close to that done by a fixed employee.

In general, it seems as if in the new capitalism of knowledge, the traditional industrial process of deskilling/devalorization of the labor force has been replaced by a process of declassement which rests in a massive way on pre-carisation. Convergence between the three dimensions of qualification recog-nized by statistical studies (individual, wage and employment) is thus broken more and more by a strategy which aims to underpay graduate employees by classifying them in professional categories lower than their qualifications and competencies, whether acquired or required.

To complete this picture of the precarisation of young people and intel-lectual work, it should not be forgotten that the majority of students, to finance their studies, must work, and, in 20% of the cases, this paid activity corre-sponds to one half-time equivalent spread out over a full year. This situation with paid work is reinforced by the fact that the young people under 25 years and students cannot benefit from the *Revenu minimum d'insertion* (RMI). This discriminatory measure ensures an abundant reserve of intermittent workers in the industrial services sector (the famous McJobs), which exploit a great quan-tity of student labor force. The figure of the student thus converges more and more with that of the working poor, putting many young people in a situation where they fail their courses. This process of precarization and impoverish-ment is worsened by two other elements:

a) Real estate speculation means that the price of access to housing, for those who are not already owners, now constitutes the main part of the total ex-penditure for a household. We have here, along with declassement and precarization, a central element of the impoverishment of the rising gen-eration of workers resulting from mass schooling;
b) The late entry to the labor market and the discontinuity of the professional career of young people (punctuated by periods of education, short con-tracts and training courses) makes access to the social security system more difficult. For most of them the possibility of enjoying a sufficiently funded retirement for even one day is already compromised.

Within this framework, the introduction of the *Contrat première embauche* (CPE) (since withdrawn by the government) and of the CNE (*Contrat nou-velle embauche*) is only the last link of a policy of progressive labor market deregulation, which goes hand in hand with the reduction of social guarantees related to the welfare state.

The common element to these two forms of employment contract is the suppression of just cause for dismissal by the establishing a probation period of two years during which the contract can be cancelled at any moment and without any justification or possibility of recourse. The only differences relate to the sectors and the categories of people to which they are applied. The CNE, which came into effect in August 2005, is applicable to all employees of companies of less than twenty people. The field of application of the CPE, on the other hand, concerned young people under 26 in companies with more than twenty paid workers.

In this context, one understands why the movement of students and precarious young people was the engine of a powerful process of social recomposition, at once intergenerational and extending across the national territory. Beginning in the universities, the anti-CPE movement quickly spread to high schools and the young people of the banlieues — the protagonists of the riots of autumn 2005, which are often wrongly stigmatized as the revolt of those excluded from the new knowledge capitalism. On this intergenerational plane, the process of recomposition finds its material base in the deterioration of living conditions for households.

In particular, while young people, who are caught within the horizon of precariousness and uncertainty, are often unable to build an autonomous existence away from the family, the awakening develops in the parents that the DCI does not protect more than one wage cut and cannot stop the multiplication of dismissals resulting from stock market fluctuations. Far from reabsorbing unemployment, which fluctuates in a structural way around the level of 10%, the neoliberal policies of flexibility and budgetary austerity put in place during the last thirty years have only generalized a feeling of insecurity in almost the whole population. At the same time, they are responsible for the stagnation of expenditure in education and research — i.e., investments in strategic knowledge from the point of view of long-term growth.

Finally, all these factors combine to explain the intensity of a social crisis whose stakes go well beyond the struggle that led to the withdrawal of the CPE.

What is certain is that the resolution to this crisis will not come about through a return to the Fordist model of labor regulation as has been proposed in a variety of ways by the majority of the French left (from socialists to Trotskyists.) The principal problem that the struggle of students and precarious workers poses (in France and across Europe) is the need for the elaboration of new labor rights and a system of social protection capable of reconciling revenue security with labor mobility. This must be done in a way that favors desired mobility rather than that imposed by employers. The welfare systems of the Nordic countries, but also those of those countries in the EU, already have in place some of the prerequisites from which this alternative model of regulation might be constructed, on the condition that there is a return to the dynamic of de-marketification of the economy by means of reinforcing the effective liberty of individuals through the labor market.

In this perspective, we can consider the putting into place of an unconditional General Guaranteed Income. From the point of view of a knowledge based economy, the General Guaranteed Income can be seen as both a collective social investment in knowledge and a primary income for individuals. That is to say, a social salary that stems directly from productive contributions and not a mere redistributive social benefit (e.g. a negative tax).

Notes on the Edu-factory
and Cognitive Capitalism

George Caffentzis and Silvia Federici

F ollowing up on our brief history of the work of the Committee for Academic Freedom in Africa (CAFA), here we share some reflections on two concepts that have been central to this discussion: the Edu-factory and cognitive capitalism.

First, we agree with the key point of the "Edu-factory " discussion prospectus:

As was the factory, so now is the university. Where once the factory was a paradigmatic site of struggle between workers and capitalists, so now the university is a key space of conflict, where the ownership of knowledge, the reproduction of the labor force, and the creation of social and cultural stratifications are all at stake. This is to say the university is not just another institution subject to sovereign and governmental controls, but a crucial site in which wider social struggles are won and lost.

CAFA's support for the struggles in African universities followed from the same analysis and logic. Universities are important places of class struggle, and not only in Europe and North America. We insisted on this point against the critics of the post-colonial university, who looked down on any effort to defend educational systems that they saw as modeled on colonial education. We argued that university struggles in Africa express a refusal to let international capital:

- decide the conditions of work;
- appropriate the wealth invested in these institution which people have paid for;
- suppress the democratization and politicization of education that on African campuses had grown through the 1980s and 90s.

More generally, in the same way as we would oppose the shutting down of factories where workers have struggled to control work and wages — especially if these workers were determined to fight against the closures — so we agree that we should resist the dismantling of public education, even though schools are also instruments of class rule and alienation. This is a contradiction that we cannot wish away and is present in all our struggles. Whether we are struggling around education, health, housing, etc. it is illusory to think that we can place ourselves outside of capitalist relations whenever we wish and from there build a new society. As students' movements across the planet have shown, universities are not just nurseries for the leaders of a neoliberal elite, they are also a terrain for debate, contestation of institutional politics, and reappropriation of resources.

It is through these debates, struggles and reappropriations, and by connecting the struggles in the campuses to the struggles in other parts of the social factory, that we create alternative forms of education and alternative educational practices. In Italy, for instance, with the contract of 1974, metal-mechanic workers were able to win 150 hours of paid study leave per year in which, together with teachers, mostly from the student movement, they organized curricula that analyzed the capitalist organization of work, also in their own workplaces. In the US, since the 60s, the campuses have been among the centers of the anti-war movement, producing a wealth of analysis about the military-industrial complex and the role of the universities in its functioning and expansion. In Africa, the university campuses were centers of resistance to structural adjustment and analysis of its implications. This is certainly one of the reasons why the World Bank was so eager to dismantle them.

The struggle in the Edu-factory is especially important today because of the strategic role of knowledge in the production system in a context in which the "enclosure" of knowledge (its privatization, commodification, expropriation through the intellectual property regimes) is a pillar of economic restructuring. We are concerned, however, that we do not overestimate this importance, and/or use the concept of the Edu-factory to set up new hierarchies with respect to labor and forms of capitalist accumulation.

This concern arises from our reading of the use that is made of the concept of "cognitive capitalism" as found in the statement circulated by Conricerca as well as in the work of some Italian autonomists. True, we need to identify the leading forms of capitalist accumulation in all its different phases, and recognize their "tendency" to hegemonize (though not to homogenize) other forms of capitalist production. But we should not dismiss the critiques of Marxian theory developed by the anti-colonial movement and the feminist movement, which have shown that capitalist accumulation has thrived precisely through its capacity to simultaneously organize development and underdevelopment, waged and un-waged labor, production at the highest levels of technological know-how and production at the lowest levels. In other words, we should not dismiss the argument that it is precisely through these disparities, the divisions built in the working class through them, and the capacity to transfer wealth/surplus from one pole to the other that capitalist accumulation has expanded in the face of so much struggle.

There are many issues involved that we can only touch upon in these notes. We want, above all, to concentrate here on the political implications of the use of the notion of "cognitive capitalism," but here are a few points for discussion.

First, the history of capitalism should demonstrate that the capitalist subsumption of all forms of production does not require the extension of the level of science and technology achieved at any particular point of capitalist development to all workers contributing to the accumulation process. It is now acknowledged, for instance, that the plantation system was organized along capitalist lines; in fact, it was a model for the factory. However, the cotton picking plantation slaves in the US South of 1850s were not working at the level of technological know-how available to workers in the textile mills of the US North of the time, though their product was a lifeline for these same mills. Does that mean that the Southern slaves were industrial workers or, vice versa, the Northern wage workers were plantation workers? Similarly, to this day, capitalism has not mechanized housework despite the fact that the unpaid domestic work of women has been a key source of accumulation for capital. Again, why at the peak of an era of "cognitive capitalism" do we witness an expansion of labor in slave-like conditions, at the lowest level of technological know-how — child labor, labor in sweatshops, labor in the new agricultural plantations and mining fields of Latin America, Africa, etc.? Can we say that workers in these conditions are "cognitive workers"? Are they and their struggles irrelevant to and/or outside the circuit of capitalist accumulation? Why has wage labor, once considered the defining form of capitalist work, still not been extended even to the majority of workers in capitalist society?

This example and these questions suggest that work can be organized for capitalist accumulation and along capitalist lines without the laborer working at the average level of technological/scientific knowledge applied in the highest points of capitalist production. They also suggest that the logic of capitalism can only be grasped by looking at the totality of its relations, and not only to the highest point of its scientific/technological achievement. Capitalism has systematically and strategically produced disparities through the international and sexual/racial division of labor and through the "underdevelopment" of particular sectors of its production, and these disparities have not been erased, but in fact have been deepened by the increasing integration of science and technology in the production process. For instance, in the era of cognitive labor, the majority of Africans do not have access to the Internet or for that matter even the telephone; even the miniscule minority who does, has access to it only for limited periods of time, because of the intermittent availability of electricity. Similarly, illiteracy, especially among women, has grown exponentially from the 1970s to present. In other words, a leap forward for many workers, has been accompanied by a leap backward by many others, who are now even more excluded from the "global discourse," and certainly not in the position to participate in global cooperation networks based upon the internet.

Second and most important are the political implications of a use of "cognitive capitalism" and "cognitive labor" that overshadows the continuing importance of other forms of work as contributors to the accumulation process.

There is the danger that by privileging one kind of capital (and therefore one kind of worker) as being the most productive, the most advanced, the most exemplary of the contemporary paradigm, etc., we create a new hierarchy of struggle, and we engage in form of activism that precludes a recomposition of the working class. Another danger is that we fail to anticipate the strategic moves by which capitalism can restructure the accumulation process by taking advantage of the inequalities within the global workforce. How the last globalization drive was achieved is exemplary in this case.

Concerning the danger of confirming in our activism the hierarchies of labor created by the extension of capitalist relations, there is much we can learn from the past. As the history of class struggle demonstrates, privileging one sector of the working class over the others is the surest road to defeat. Undoubtedly, certain types of workers have played a crucial role in certain historical phases of capitalist development. But the working class has paid a very high price to a revolutionary logic that established hierarchies of revolutionary subjects, patterned on the hierarchies of the capitalist organization of work. Marxist/socialist activists in Europe lost sight of the revolutionary power of the world's "peasantry." More than that, peasant movements have been destroyed (see the case of the ELAS in Greece) by communists who considered only the factory worker as organizable and "truly revolutionary." Socialists/marxists also lost sight of the immense (house) work that was being done to produce and reproduce industrial workers. The huge "iceberg" of labor in capitalism (to use Maria Mies' metaphor) was made invisible by the tendency to look at the tip of the iceberg, industrial labor, while the labor involved in the reproduction of labor-power went unseen, with the result that the feminist movement was often fought against and seen as something outside the class struggle.

Ironically, under the regime of industrial capitalism and factory work, it was the peasant movements of Mexico, China, Cuba, Vietnam, and to a great extent Russia who made the revolutions of the 20th century. In the 1960s as well, the impetus for change at the global level came from the anti-colonial struggle, including the struggle against apartheid and for Black Power in the United States. Today, it is the indigenous people, the campesinos, the unemployed of Mexico (Chiapas, Oaxaca), Bolivia, Ecuador, Brazil, Venezuela, the farmers of India, the maquila workers of the US border, the immigrant workers of the US, etc. who are conducting the most "advanced" struggles against the global extension of capitalist relations.

Let us be very clear. We make these points not to minimize the importance of the struggles in the Edu-factory and the ways in which the Internet has led to the creation of new kinds of commons that are crucial to our struggle, but because we fear we may repeat mistakes that may ultimately isolate those who work and struggle in these networks. From this viewpoint, we think that the "no-global" movement (for all its difficulties) was a step forward in its capacity to articulate demands and forms of activism that projected the struggle in a global way, creating a new type of internationalism, one bringing together computer programmers, artists, and other edu-workers in one movement, each making its distinctive contribution.

For this political *re-composition* to become possible, however, we need to see the continuity of our struggle through the difference of our places in the international division of labor, and to articulate our demands and strategies in accordance to these differences and the need to overcome them. Assuming that a recomposition of the workforce is already occurring because work is becoming homogenized — through a process that some have defined as the "becoming common of labor" — will not do. We cannot cast the "cognitive" net so widely that almost every kind of work becomes "cognitive" labor, short of making arbitrary social equations and obfuscating our understanding of what is new about "cognitive labor" in the present phase of capitalism.

It is an arbitrary move (for instance) to assimilate, under the "cognitive" label, the work of a domestic worker — whether an immigrant or not, whether s/he is a wife/mother/sister or a paid laborer — to that of a computer programmer or computer artist and, on top of it, suggest that the cognitive aspect of domestic work is something new, owing to the dominance of a new type of capitalism.

Certainly domestic work, like every form of reproductive work, does have a strong cognitive component. To know how to adjust the pillows under the body of a sick person so that the skin does not blister and the bones do not hurt is a science and an art that requires much attention, knowledge and experimentation. The same is true of the care for a child, and of most other aspects of "housework" whoever may be doing this work. But it is precisely when we look at the vast universe of practices that constitute reproductive work, especially when performed in the home, that we see the limits of the application of the type of computer-based, technological know-how on which "cognitive capitalism relies." We see that the knowledge necessary for reproductive work can certainly benefit from the use of the Internet (assuming there is time and money for it), but it is one type of knowledge that human beings, mostly women, have developed over a long period of time, in conformity with but also against the requirements of the capitalist organization of work.

We should add that nothing is gained by admitting housework into the new realm of cognitive labor, by redefining is as "affective labor" or, as some have done, "immaterial labor," or again "care work." For a start, we should avoid formulas that imply a body/mind, reason/emotion separation in any type of work and its products.

Moreover, does replacing the notion of "reproductive work," as used by the feminist movement, with that of "affective labor" truly serve to assimilate, under the "cognitive" label, the work of a domestic worker (whether immigrant or not, whether a wife/sister/mother or paid laborer) or the work of a sex worker to that of a computer programmer or computer artist? What is really "common" in their labor, taking into account all the complex of social relations sustaining their different forms of work? What is common, for instance, between a male computer programmer or artist or teacher and a female domestic worker who, in addition to having a paid job, must also spend many hours doing unpaid labor taking care of her family members? (Immigrant women too often have family members to care for in the countries to which they migrate, or must send part of their salary home to pay for those caring for their family members.)

Most crucial of all, if the labor involved in the reproduction of human beings — still an immense part of the labor expended in capitalist society — is "cognitive," in the sense that it produces not things but "states of being," then, what is new about "cognitive labor"? And, equally important, what is gained by assimilating all forms of work — even as a tendency — under one label, except that some kinds of work and the political problematic they generate again disappear?

Isn't the case that by stating that domestic work is "cognitive work" we fail, once again, to address the question of the devaluation of this work in capitalist society, its largely unpaid status, the gender hierarchies that are built upon it, and through the wage relation? Shouldn't we ask, instead, what kind of organizing can be done — so that domestic workers and computer programmers can come together — rather than assuming that we all becoming assimilated in the *mare magnum* of "cognitive labor"?

Taking reproductive work as a standard also serves to question the prevailing assumption that the cognitivization of work, in the sense of its computerization / reorganization through the Internet — has an emancipatory effect. A voluminous feminist literature has challenged the idea that the industrialization of many aspects of housework has reduced housework time for women. In fact, many studies have shown that industrialization has increased the range of what is considered as socially necessary housework. The same is true with the infiltration of science and technology into domestic work, including childcare and sex work. For example, the spread of personal computers, for those houseworkers who can afford them and have time to use them, can help relieve the isolation and monotony of housework through chat rooms and social networks. But the creation of virtual communities does not alleviate the increasing problem of loneliness, nor helps the struggle against the destruction of community bonds and the proliferation of gated worlds.

In conclusion, notions like "cognitive labor" and "cognitive capitalism" should be used with the understanding that they represent a part, though a leading one, of capitalist development and that different forms of knowledge and cognitive work exist that cannot be flattened under one label. Short of that, the very utility of such concepts in identifying what is new in capitalist accumulation and the struggle against it is lost. What is also lost is the fact that, far from communalizing labor, every new turn in capitalist development tends to deepen the divisions in the world proletariat, and that as long as these divisions exist they can be used to reorganize capital on a different basis and destroy the terrain on which movements have grown.

Translation, Biopolitics
and Colonial Difference
Naoki Sakai and Jon Solomon

he primary imperative given to subjective formation under the post-
Fordist regime of immaterial labor is, as Maurizio Lazzarato and Toni
Negri observed nearly two decades ago, communication. An imperative that might seem like a moment of opening turns in fact into just the opposite: "The [post-Fordist] subject," writes Lazzarato, "is a simple relay of
codification and decodification, whose transmitted message must be 'clear and
without ambiguity,' within a context of communication that has been completely normalized." In the context of the new global economy and its migratory regimes, subjects of communication face the especially daunting task of
accounting for enormous differences and diversities throughout and across
global populations. Hence, if communication is to be effective, it requires an
ideology of anthropological difference according to which the normalization
of diverse populations can be universally instituted. Needless to say, in the era
of post-colonial governance, such normalization would encounter impossible
resistance were it to proceed according to a model of uniformity that would inevitably highlight the uneven relations between center and periphery. What is
needed, rather, is a strategy of normalization that accounts for and includes
difference, yet organizes it according to predictable codes. Amidst the litany of
various biologico-sociological classificatory schemes that have arisen — often
with disastrous political consequences — since the 19th century, none is more
pervasive, historically persistent and considered to be politically neutral than
that of "culture." Culture provides communication with the crucial classificatory framework necessary both to preserve difference at a level acceptable to
post-colonial governance and to ensure sufficient regularity in codification.

According to this representational scheme, "translation" names the process of encoding/decoding required to transfer informational content between different linguistico-cultural spheres. Just as the post-Fordist subject must "communicate," the nature of "communication" itself is strictly codified according to a grammar of pronominal identities and representational positions that codifies linguistic exchange according to an essentially predetermined representational scheme of mutually determined anthropological codes.

In contemporary parlance, "cultural translation" names the ostensibly ethical relation to the other founded on mutual respect for difference. Given the massive effects of lingering colonial difference, according to which "the West" is supposed to exercise a dominating mediation upon cultural representations across the globe, "cultural translation" undoubtedly constitutes an irrefutably progressive development in the recognition of previously colonized peoples. Yet as Boris Buden points out in his defense of "strategic essentialism," the notion of translation utilized by today's proponents of cultural translation is not the conventional, modernist one that emphasizes semantic identity and hierarchies of translatability and untranslatability, but rather a postmodernist one sensitive to the problems of indeterminacy and difference raised by the philosophies of difference.

In 2006, we published an issue of the multilingual series *Traces* titled "Translation, Biopolitics, Colonial Difference" in which we presented an argument for articulating the indeterminacy of translation as a modality of social practice to the contingent commodifications of labor-power and the nexus of knowledge that governs anthropological difference. The call for papers for that issue proposed to prospective authors the idea of bringing translation squarely into a politically informed discussion about the production of both social relations and humanistic knowledge in the context of anthropological difference inherited from colonialism. We did not hide our ambition to push the idea of cultural translation beyond "strategic essentialism" to present a new vision of syncretic knowledge and social practice that would directly subvert the anthropo-technological status of "the West" as both exception and a form of immunity. Central to this discussion was the notion of a biopolitics of translation. In a series of lectures in the late 1970s, Michel Foucault introduced and elaborated the assorted concepts of "biopolitics" and "governmentality" as tools for thinking about the way in which the processes of life — and the possibility of controlling and modifying them through the technical means — enter the sphere of power and become its chief concern. Foucault's effort has generally been understood as an innovative attempt to introduce a new ontology, beginning with the body, that would provide a way of thinking the political subject outside the dominant tradition of modern political philosophy that frames it as a subject of law. "Biopolitics" thus names a quotidian sphere of ostensibly apolitical (or depoliticized) social action and relations — what Foucault calls "the entry of life into history" — that is nevertheless invested with crucial effects for the production of social subjects. These effects, far removed from the role traditionally ascribed to politics per se, nevertheless bear directly upon the construction of what is at stake in the formation of power relations.

In order to use tools from Foucault's conceptual kit, however, we found it was not only possible but also necessary to subject the latent and pervasive Occidentalism in his work to a thorough critique while at the same time opening up possibilities for an understanding of biopolitics in a global context. The notion of a "biopolitics of translation" acquires conceptual validity and critical importance with a view to the specifically modern — which is to say, global — phenomenon of the linguistic standardization associated with nationalization and colonial land appropriation. Ever since the concomitant birth of philology and biology, modernity has been associated with the advent of a global cartographic imaginary that places peoples with no prior "memory" of migratory contact, or only "deep memory" such as etymology, into relation through the mediation of an imperial center. As the transition to a global form of spatial imaginary, modernity begins, linguistically speaking, when the project of standardization is extended across all manner of social differences to encompass diverse populations in the process of national homogenization (which occurs, as Jacques Bidet argues, on the level of world system) and domestic segmentation (which occurs on the level of "class" difference or structure). This process must be seen, in turn, in the context of contact with other global populations undergoing the same traumatic process of systemic definition and structural segmentation. The biopolitics of translation thus names that space of exchange and accumulation in which politics appears to have been preempted by the everyday occurrence of language. Our research shows that when "translation" is understood according to a representational scheme of the epistemtic subject, it names not the operation by which cultural difference is "bridged," but rather the preemptive operation through which originary difference — what is encountered when translation is understood as an act of social practice — is segmented and organized according to the various classificatory schemes of biologico-sociological knowledge emerging out of the colonial encounter.

Seen from this perspective, the modern regime of translation is a concrete form of "systemic complicity" whose primary function is population management within the purview of imperial domination. In other words, it is a globally-applicable technique of segmentation aimed at managing social relationships by forcing them to pass through circuits on the "systemic" level. In our research on the transnational discursive structure of both Japanese studies and the institution of the Japanese Emperor system, or again in the relation between imperial nationalism and the maintenance of ethnic minorities, we were persuaded that the geography of national sovereignty and civilizational difference that constitutes the geocultural and geopolitical map of both the world and the human sciences indicates an important kind of subjective technology or governmental technique that has, until recently, been thoroughly naturalized by an anthropological discourse of "culture." It is only today that we can begin to see how a multiplicity of disciplinary arrangements forming an economy of translation (in place since the colonial era but far outliving colonialism's demise) actually produces differentially coded subjects, typically national/racial ones, whose constitution is interdependent and, at specific intervals, actually complicit in a single, yet extremely hierarchical, state of domination. Our aim was thus to trace a series of genealogies within which "translation" is no longer seen as simply an operation of transfer, relay, and equivalency, but rather assumes a vital historical role in the constitution of the social.

Our research into the position of the translator within the modern regime of co-figured, nationalized language, shows a precise parallel to the logic of sovereignty. Just as Giorgio Agamben has shown how sovereignty is based on the form of exception (embodied by the figure of the sovereign), the position of the translator in the modern era has been represented in a similarly exceptional fashion. Our work has turned this relationship inside out, demonstrating that the regularity of the "national language" as a formation in which the (hybrid) position of the translator has been deemed irrelevant is in fact produced in a representational manner only after the practical encounter of social difference in translation. By proposing to look at the formation of national language through the ostensibly exceptional case of translation, we have been able to show that it is indeed a systemic, or international, technique of domination. This discovery parallels the growing awareness, largely advanced by Yann Moulier Boutang, of the crucial role in capitalist expansion played by the various forms of irregular and slave labor, rather than the regularized forms of wage labor. Hence, at the back of the call for papers for that issue was a proposal to displace the state of domination managed by the dual normalizing technologies of wage labor and nationalized speaking subjects with the inventive subjectivities seen in the exodus from wage labor and national language. In effect, translation appears to us as the social relation from which the critique of communication and its corollary "culture" as the reigning ideology of capital is most directly linked to a politics of life, or again, the politics in which life becomes invested by capital.

In the various exceptions that alternately govern labor, life and language, we begin to grasp the way in which "the West" has established and maintained its "identity" as a specter for the last few centuries as the leading, knowledgeable region of the globe that supposedly exports innovation and development to other regions. Yet the very concept of the global, according to which regions as such are imagined is intrinsically indebted to the legacy of colonialism. Although the colonial encounter produced the first truly global relation, "the West" identified itself as a particular and unique region only by claiming exemptive subtraction from this relation while at the same time undertaking unprecedented accumulation through originary expropriation.

The contemporary configuration of the West and the Rest along an immunitarian model is but the most recent development in this remarkably durable history. As the contemporary West prepares to innoculate itself against a slew of viral threats supposedly emanating from the Third World, it is well worth remembering that for the indigenous, pre-Columbian populations of the "New World," the contact with Europeans brought far more death from disease than any other cause. It took nearly 400 years, we are told, for population levels in North and South America to reach pre-Columbian levels. This decimation of pre-Columbian populations by viral disease, often occurring in advance of actual contact with Conquistadors and European colonists, constitutes an emblematic event of modernity: here, we find the original form of immunitarian distance that disavows the destructive, expropriative relationship while subsequently preserving the account of that history in the codes of anthropological difference. The temporal inversion effected by the representation of this event is what authorizes the West to claim its "sane and civilizing" mission and repress its viral, barbaric history.

The presentation to the Multitudes list of our call for a biopolitics of translation requires more elaboration than we can provide here, but we would like minimally to address two points: 1) If "co-figuration" names the structure of the world inasmuch as anthropological difference is governed by the epistemological representation of translation (at the expense of the practical subject), then it could be politically-pertinent to see something like a European reception of this project. *Vis-à-vis* the global networks of bipolarity established by the United States (which remains dominant in Asia), Europe stands in a highly ambivalent position. Undoubtedly some Europeans will dream of making this cause for a new European exception. But at the same time, this "rift in Empire," to borrow Brian Holmes's suggestive phrase, also presents us with an interesting possibility to displace the bipolarity. 2) Concomitant with this creative potential, we cannot overemphasize the necessity of a long-term, far-reaching critique, via the conceptual framework of translation, of the Eurocentrism and Occidentalism that still pervades the Human Sciences today. Previous critiques of Occidentalism have focused on themes such as colonial ambivalency and the reversal of established hierarchies, yet tend to leave the basic structure of anthropological difference intact inasmuch as it is linguistically-encoded in the complex and mobile relations between major and minor languages; by contrast, a project in the biopolitics of translation brings to the critique of the West both an epistemological critique of the anthropological basis of knowledge and a practical engagement with the contemporary social formation at the level of expression. Just as the Marxian critique of the commodity fetish proposed to remind us that the fruits of labor, now reified, actually bear within them the trace of a social relation (and hence the possibility of creative transformation), we advance the thesis that translation can also be understood as a form of social relation requiring similar critique of elements assumed to be extraneous to the production of meaning and bearing similar creative potential. From the geneaological perspective of a biopolitics of translation, the emphasis is on, as Negri and Hardt propose of the multitude, not what we are but rather what we can become.

Crucial to that potentiality in the post-Fordist era is what Foucault would call the role of the "specific intellectual." If anthropological difference coded as "translation" (understood, once again, according to an epistemico-representational scheme rather than as a modality of social practice) is the reigning ideology of the post-Fordist imperative to communicate, one must pay particular attention to the way the subject of knowledge, formed in the crucible of disciplinary and linguistic codifications still indebted to the legacy of colonial difference, is particularly prone to communicate according to a restricted economy of ressentiment. This is not so much a problem of colonial psychology in the Fanonian sense, but rather a more generally encompassing economy of subjective formation distinguished by the structure of return and the contradictions that riddle the search for recognition by minorities.

Undoubtedly, the struggle for control over the representational tactics of anthropological difference, as it plays out within and between disciplines as well as within and between nationalized populations favors the production of subjects bound by the expression of ressentiment. Control over the codification of this representational scheme invariably involves preemptively identifying with an exceptional position that is subsequently disavowed even while actively promoting its creation through disciplinary institutions. It is within this historical context that we can fruitfully expand upon Lazzarato and Negri's seminal observation that the role of the intellectual today "ne peut donc être réduite ni à une fonction épistémologique et critique, ni à un engagement et à un témoignage de libération: c'est au niveau de l'agencement collectif même qu'il intervient [cannot thus be reduced either to an epistemological and critical function, nor to an engagement with and witness to liberation]." Within the biopolitics of translation, the construction of collective agency occurs each time anew in what our research has called the mode of the heterolingual address: in this mode, as we have said before, "you are always confronted, so to speak, with foreigners in your enunciation when your attitude is that of the heterolingual address. Precisely because you wish to communicate with her, him, or them, so the first, and perhaps most fundamental, determination of your addressee, is that of the one who might not comprehend your language, that is, of the foreigner."

We propose, in closing, to see in the biopolitics of translation the form of social movement that corresponds most specifically to the intellectual laborer of today — a practice of knowledge, in other words, as a social movement of "permanent translation " (to use Rada Ivekovic's brilliantly succinct formulation) devoted to producing the multitude of foreigners we can become. It is perhaps only from this perspective that one can still hope, in this era of globalized civil war and unresolved historical injustice, for forms of collective agency capable of constituting a decisive break with the political subject of ressentiment.

PART IV

The Production of the Common and the Global Autonomous University

A Hierarchy of Networks?
or, Geo-Culturally Differentiated Networks
and the Limits of Collaboration

Ned Rossiter

How to think the passage from hierarchisation to autonomous institutions? Indeed, I think it appropriate to maintain the connection between hierarchy and autonomy. This constitutive tension is apparent in the political economy and social-technical dimensions of both open source and proprietary software that provides the architecture for communicative relations. And it manifests on multiple fronts in the modalities of organization that attend the creation of autonomous times and spaces of radical or alternative research and education projects, experiments and agendas. There is no absolute autonomy, but rather a complex field of forces and relations that hold the potential for partial autonomy, or "the difference which makes a difference" (Bateson). How to move and direct such complexities in such a way that makes possible autonomous education is what I understand to be the program of Edu-factory .

And in such guidance — a combination of collective investigation and top-down decision-making — one finds the movement between hierarchy and autonomy. This is a matter of governance for networks. Protocols come in to play, and dispute, disagreement and alliance shape the culture of networks in singular ways. At the technical level, there are some near universal features of networks: TCP/IP, location of root-servers according to the geo-politics of information, adoption of open source and/or proprietary software, allocation of domain names, etc. But as the debates around the UN's World Summit on the

Information Society (2003-2005) amply demonstrated, it quickly becomes analytically and politically implausible to separate the technical aspects of information from social and cultural conditions. Autonomous education that makes use of ICTs will always be situated within a geography of uneven information. Hierarchies will always prevail.

The possibility of transnational collaboration that aspires to autonomous education thus becomes a problem of translation, as Jon Solomon and others have discussed in rich ways on the Edu-factory mailing list. There will be no "construction of an autonomous global university." How, then, might autonomous education initiatives undergo scalar transformations in such a way that make transnational relations possible? This seems to be the ambition of the Edu-factory . But what is the desire for transnational connection? Why not keep things local, rooted in the geographies of the city, neighborhood or village? Who is the subject of, let us say, not a global but transnational education project that resides sufficiently outside the corporate university?

Part of the brilliance of the edu-Summit held in Berlin in May, 2007, was to finally break with the anti- or alter-globalization cycle of staging protests according to the diary of the WTO, G8, etc.[1] Autonomy begins with invention that is co-emergent with conflict, crisis, frustration, curiosity, depression, wild utopian desires, boredom, etc. The sites of conflict are multiple: individual, institutional, social/collective, corporeal, affective, ecological, cultural, disciplinary, geopolitical, governmental, etc. Underscored by heterolingual tensions and incommensurabilities, the Edu-factory organizers' call for and presupposition of "the realization of our collective project" is nothing short of complex (a problematic acknowledged by Edu-factory organizers and participants). But one needs to take care not to allow complexity to displace the conflict that takes place in occupying a line or position. This is the space of the political.

What is the situation of autonomous institutions? Paolo Do: "Talking about an autonomous university is to find a starting-point to attack and to occupy the spaces belonging to the enemy."[2] Such an approach is a reactionary one if it is to be reduced to a takeover, say, of the institutional spaces of the university. The conservative tendency in such a move lies in a responsive mechanism determined by the space and time of "the enemy," or hegemonic institution (the university as we know it). To simply occupy the spaces of the enemy is to repeat the failure Foucault saw of revolution: the end-result is a reproduction of the same. This amounts to a reformist agenda and, in the case of the transformation of universities over the past 20 or so years, succeeds in the production and proliferation of managerial subjectivities.

There are, however, different registers of occupation, and I will assume this to be the interest of Paolo. A good example can be found in the case of domestic workers in Hong Kong and their invention of new institutional forms that arise through the practice of occupation. The potential for commonalities across laboring bodies is undoubtedly a complex and often fraught subjective and institutional process or formation. The fractured nature of working times, places and practices makes political organization highly difficult. Where this does happen, there are often ethnic affinities coalesced around specific sectors — here, we are thinking of examples such as the "Justice for Janitors" movement in the US, a largely Latino immigrant experience of self-organization.[3]

In Hong Kong, domestic workers gather on Sundays within non-spaces such as road fly-overs, under pedestrian bridges and in public parks. The domestics are female workers for the most part, initially from the Philippines with a new wave of workers in recent years from Indonesia, Malaysia and Thailand.[4] And as cultural critic Helen Grace notes, "there are also mainland migrant workers with limited rights, working in all sorts of low-paid jobs, moving backwards and forwards and living with great precarity."[5]

The domestic workers transform the status of social-ethnic borders by occupying spaces from which they are usually excluded due to the spatial and temporal constraints of labor. Sunday is the day off for domestic workers, and they don't want to stay at home, nor do their employers wish to have them about the house. The Norman Foster designed headquarters for HSBC bank located in Central district nicely encapsulates the relation between domestic workers and capital and the disconnection between state and citizen. This bank is just one of many instances found globally where the corporate sector makes available public spaces in the constitution of an "entrepreneurial city."[6]

Yet the actions of undocumented workers mark a distinction from the entrepreneurial city and its inter-scalar strategies of capital accumulation in the form of property development and business, financial, IT and tourist services. With a first floor of public space, workers engage in praying and study groups reading the Koran, singing songs, labor organization, cutting hair and dancing while finance capital is transferred in floors above the floating ceiling of the HSBC bank. Used in innovative ways that conflict with or at least depart from how these spaces usually function, there is a correspondence here with what Grace calls a "horizontal monumentality," "making highly visible — and public — a particular aspect of otherwise privatized labor and domestic space."[7]

Not described in tourist guides and absent from policy and corporate narratives of entrepreneurial innovation and development, the domestic worker is a public without a discourse. For many Hong Kong residents their visibility is undesirable, yet these workers make a significant contribution to the city's imaginary: their visibility on Sundays signals that the lustre of entrepreneurialism is underpinned by highly insecure and low-paid forms of work performed by non-citizens. The domestic worker also instantiates less glamorous but nonetheless innovative forms of entrepreneurialism. An obvious example here consists of the small business initiatives such as restaurants, delis and small-scale repairs and manufacturing that some migrant workers go on to develop, making way for new intakes of domestic workers in the process and redefining the ethnic composition of the city. Such industriousness provides an important service to local residents and contributes in key ways to the social-cultural fabric of the city.

The competition of urban space — particularly the use of urban space — by the domestic worker also comprises an especially innovative act: the invention of a new institutional form, one that we call the "organized network." The transnational dimension of the domestic workers is both external and internal. External, in their return home every year or two for a week or so — a passage determined by the time of labor and festivity (there is little need for domestics during the Chinese New Year). Internal, with respect to the composition of the group itself. In this case, there exists "a multiplicity of overlapping sites that are themselves internally heterogeneous."8 Here, I am thinking of the borders of sociality that compose the gathering of domestics in one urban setting or another — as mentioned above, some choose to sing, engage in labor organization, hold study groups, etc. Ethnic and linguistic differences also underscore the internal borders of the group.

Can the example of domestic workers in Hong Kong be understood in terms of a transnational organized network? I suspect not. The domestics only meet in particular times and spaces (Sunday in urban non-spaces). Such a form of localization obviously does not lend itself to transnational connection. Perhaps NGOs and social movements that rally around the conditions of domestic workers communicate within a transnational network of organizations engaged in similar advocacy work. But if this is the case, then we are speaking of a different register of subjectivity and labor — one defined by the option of expanded choice and self-determination.

In this sense, we can identify a hierarchy of networks whose incommensurabilities are of a scalar nature: local as distinct from transnational. For domestic workers, much of this has to do with external conditions over which they have little control: Sunday is the day off work, exile from their country of origin is shaped by lack of economic options and the forces of global capital, their status as undocumented or temporary workers prevents equivalent freedom of movement and political rights afforded by Hong Kong citizens, etc. But within these constraints, invention is possible.

Part one of this second round of discussions on the Edu-factory mailing list identified many of the conditions at work that shape the differential experience of labor and practices of education. How to make the transition to institution strikes me as the task now at hand.

Notes

Parts of this text are drawn from a forthcoming article: Brett Neilson and Ned Rossiter (2008), "Precarity as a Political Concept, or, Fordism as Exception," *Theory, Culture & Society,* Nottingham, v. 25 n.7 .

1. Summit: Non-Aligned Initiatives in Education Culture, Berlin, 24-28 May, 2007, http://summit.kein.org

2. Paolo DFo, "Open University," post to Edu-factory list, 14 January, 2008 http://listcultures.org/pipermail/Edu-factory_listcultures.org/2008-January/000113.html

3. See Florian Schneider, "Organizing the Unorganizables," 2002, http://wastun.org/v2v/Organizing_the_Unorganizable

4. See Nicole Constable (1999), "At Home but Not at Home: Filipina Narratives of Ambivalent Returns," *Cultural Anthropology,* v. 14, n. 2 : 203-228; and Lisa Law, (2002) "Defying Disappearance: Cosmopolitan Public Spaces in Hong Kong," *Urban Studies* v. 39. n. 9: 1625–1646.

5. Helen Grace, personal email, 15 January, 2008.

6. See Bob Jessop and Ngai-Ling Sum (no date), "An Entrepreneurial City in Action: Hong Kong's Emerging Strategies in and for (Inter-)Urban Competition," http://www2.cddc.vt.edu/digitalfordism/fordism_materials/jessop.htm

7. Helen Grace (2007), "Monuments and the Face of Time: Distortions of Scale and Asynchrony in Postcolonial Hong Kong," *Postcolonial Studies* v. 10, n.4 : 469.

8. Sandro Mezzadra and Brett Neilson (2008), "Border as Method, or, the Multiplication of Labor," *transversal*, http://eipcp.net/transversal/0608/mezzadraneilson/en.

The University and the Undercommons

Stefano Harney and Fred Moten

"To the university I'll steal, and there I'll steal," to borrow from Pistol at the end of *Henry V,* as he would surely borrow from us. This is the only possible relationship to the American university today. This may be true of universities everywhere. It may have to be true of the university in general. But certainly, this much is true in the United States: it cannot be denied that the university is a place of refuge, and it cannot be accepted that the university is a place of enlightenment. In the face of these conditions one can only sneak into the university and steal what one can. To abuse its hospitality, to spite its mission, to join its refugee colony, its gypsy encampment, to be in but not of this is the path of the subversive intellectual in the modern university.

The Only Possible Relationship to the University Today Is a Criminal One

"Philosophy thus traditionally practices a critique of knowledge which is simultaneously a denegation of knowledge (i.e., of the class struggle). Its position can be described as an irony with regard to knowledge, which it puts into question without ever touching its foundations. The questioning of knowledge in philosophy always ends in its restoration: a movement great philosophers consistently expose in each other." — Jacques Rancière

"I am a black man number one, because I am against what they have done and are still doing to us; and number two, I have something to say about the new society to be built because I have a tremendous part in that which they have sought to discredit." — C. L. R. James

Worry about the university. This is the injunction today in the United States, one with a long history. Call for its restoration like Harold Bloom or Stanley Fish or Gerald Graff. Call for its reform like Derek Bok or Bill Readings or Cary Nelson. Call out to it as it calls to you. But for the subversive intellectual, all of this goes on upstairs, in polite company, among the rational men. After all, the subversive intellectual came under false pretenses, with bad documents, out of love. Her labor is as necessary as it is unwelcome. The university needs what she bears but cannot bear what she brings. And on top of all that, she disappears. She disappears into the underground, the downlow lowdown maroon community of the university, into the Undercommons of Enlightenment, where the work gets done, where the work gets subverted, where the revolution is still black, still strong.

What is that work and what is its social capacity for both reproducing the university and producing fugitivity? If one were to say teaching, one would be performing the work of the university. Teaching is merely a profession and an operation of what Jacques Derrida calls the onto-/auto encyclopedic circle of the Universitas. But it is useful to invoke this operation to glimpse the hole in the fence where labor enters, to glimpse its hiring hall, its night quarters. The university needs teaching labor, despite itself, or as itself, self-identical with and thereby erased by it. It is not teaching then that holds this social capacity, but something that produces the not visible other side of teaching, a thinking through the skin of teaching toward a collective orientation to the knowledge object as future project, and a commitment to what we want to call the prophetic organization.

But it is teaching that brings us in. Before there are grants, research, conferences, books, and journals; there is the experience of being taught and of teaching. Before the research post with no teaching, before the graduate students to mark the exams, before the string of sabbaticals, before the permanent reduction in teaching load, the appointment to run the Center, the consignment of pedagogy to a discipline called education, before the course designed to be a new book, teaching happened. The moment of teaching for food is therefore often mistakenly taken to be a stage, as if eventually, one should not teach for food. If the stage persists, there is a social pathology in the university. But if the teaching is successfully passed on, the stage is surpassed, and teaching is consigned to those who are known to remain in the stage, the sociopathological labor of the university. Kant interestingly calls such a stage "self-incurred minority." He tries to contrast it with having the "determination and courage to use one's intelligence without being guided by another." "Have the courage to use your own intelligence." But what would it mean if teaching or rather what we might call "the beyond of teaching" is precisely what one is asked to get beyond, to stop taking sustenance? And what of those minorities who refuse, the tribe of moles who will not come back from beyond (that which is beyond "the beyond of teaching"), as if they will not be subjects, as if they want to think as objects, as minority? Certainly, the perfect subjects of communication, those successfully beyond teaching, will see them as waste. But their collective labor will always call into question who truly is taking the orders of the Enlightenment. The waste lives for those moments beyond teaching when you give away the unexpected beautiful phrase unexpected, no one has asked, beautiful, it will never come back. Is being the biopower of the Enlightenment truly better than this?

Perhaps the biopower of the Enlightenment know this, or perhaps it is just reacting to the objecthood of this labor as it must. But even as it depends on these moles, these refugees, they will call them uncollegial, impractical, naive, unprofessional. And one may be given one last chance to be pragmatic why steal when one can have it all, they will ask. But if one hides from this interpellation, neither agrees nor disagrees but goes with hands full into the underground of the university, into the Undercommons this will be regarded as theft, as a criminal act. And it is at the same time, the only possible act.

In that Undercommons of the university one can see that it is not a matter of teaching versus research or even the beyond of teaching versus the individualization of research. To enter this space is to inhabit the ruptural and enraptured disclosure of the commons that fugitive enlightenment enacts, the criminal, matricidal, queer, in the cistern, on the stroll of the stolen life, the life stolen by enlightenment and stolen back, where the commons give refuge, where the refuge gives commons. What the beyond of teaching is really about is not finishing oneself, not passing, not completing; it's about allowing subjectivity to be unlawfully overcome by others, a radical passion and passivity such that one becomes unfit for subjection, because one does not possess the kind of agency that can hold the regulatory forces of subjecthood, and one cannot initiate the auto-interpellative torque that biopower subjection requires and rewards. It is not so much the teaching as it is the prophecy in the organization of the act of teaching. The prophecy that predicts its own organization and has therefore passed, as commons, and the prophecy that exceeds its own organization and therefore as yet can only be organized. Against the prophetic organization of the Undercommons is arrayed its own deadening labor for the university, and beyond that, the negligence of professionalization, and the professionalization of the critical academic. The Undercommons is therefore always an unsafe neighborhood.

Fredric Jameson reminds the university of its dependence on "Enlightenment-type critiques and demystification of belief and committed ideology, in order to clear the ground for unobstructed planning and 'development.'" This is the weakness of the university, the lapse in its homeland security. It needs labor power for this "enlightenment-type critique," but, somehow, labor always escapes.

The premature subjects of the Undercommons took the call seriously, or had to be serious about the call. They were not clear about planning, too mystical, too full of belief. And yet this labor force cannot reproduce itself, it must be reproduced. The university works for the day when it will be able to rid itself, like capital in general, of the trouble of labor. It will then be able to reproduce a labor force that understands itself as not only unnecessary but dangerous to the development of capitalism. Much pedagogy and scholarship is already dedicated in this direction. Students must come to see themselves as the problem, which, counter to the complaining of restorationist critics of the university, is precisely what it means to be a customer, to take on the burden of realization and always necessarily be inadequate to it. Later, these students will be able to see themselves properly as obstacles to society, or perhaps, with lifelong learning, students will return having successfully diagnosed themselves as the problem.

Still, the dream of an undifferentiated labor that knows itself as superfluous is interrupted precisely by the labor of clearing away the burning roadblocks of ideology. While it is better that this police function be in the hands of the few, it still raises labor as difference, labor as the development of other labor, and therefore labor as a source of wealth. And although the enlightenment-type critique, as we suggest below, informs on, kisses the cheek of, any autonomous development as a result of this difference in labor, there is a break in the wall here, a shallow place in the river, a place to land under the rocks. The university still needs this clandestine labor to prepare this undifferentiated labor force, whose increasing specialization and managerialist tendencies, again contra the restorationists, represent precisely the successful integration of the division of labor with the universe of exchange that commands restorationist loyalty.

Introducing this labor upon labor, and providing the space for its development, creates risks. Like the colonial police force recruited unwittingly from guerrilla neighborhoods, university labor may harbor refugees, fugitives, renegades, and castaways. But there are good reasons for the university to be confident that such elements will be exposed or forced underground. Precautions have been taken, book lists have been drawn up, teaching observations conducted, invitations to contribute made. Yet against these precautions stands the immanence of transcendence, the necessary deregulation and the possibilities of criminality and fugitivity that labor upon labor requires. Maroon communities of composition teachers, mentorless graduate students, adjunct Marxist historians, out or queer management professors, state college ethnic studies departments, closed-down film programs, visa-expired Yemeni student newspaper editors, historically black college sociologists, and feminist engineers. And what will the university say of them? It will say they are unprofessional. This is not an arbitrary charge. It is the charge against the more than professional. How do those who exceed the profession, who exceed and by exceeding escape, how do those maroons problematize themselves, problematize the university, force the university to consider them a problem, a danger? The Undercommons is not, in short, the kind of fanciful communities of whimsy invoked by Bill Readings at the end of his book. The Undercommons, its maroons, are always at war, always in hiding.

There Is No Distinction between the American University and Professionalization

But surely if one can write something on the surface of the university, if one can write for instance in the university about singularities those events that refuse either the abstract or individual category of the bourgeois subject one cannot say that there is no space in the university itself? Surely there is some space here for a theory, a conference, a book, a school of thought? Surely the university also makes thought possible? Is not the purpose of the university as Universitas, as liberal arts, to make the commons, make the public, make the nation of democratic citizenry? Is it not therefore important to protect this Universitas, whatever its impurities, from professionalization in the university? But we would ask what is already not possible in this talk in the hallways, among the buildings, in rooms of the university about possibility? How is the thought of the outside, as Gayatri Spivak means it, already not possible in this complaint?

The maroons know something about possibility. They are the condition of possibility of production of knowledge in the university the singularities against the writers of singularity, the writers who write, publish, travel, and speak. It is not merely a matter of the secret labor upon which such space is lifted, though of course such space is lifted from collective labor and by it. It is rather that to be a critical academic in the university is to be against the university, and to be against the university is always to recognize it and be recognized by it, and to institute the negligence of that internal outside, that unassimilated underground, a negligence of it that is precisely, we must insist, the basis of the professions. And this act of against always already excludes the unrecognized modes of politics, the beyond of politics already in motion, the discredited criminal para-organization, what Robin Kelley might refer to as the infrapolitical field (and its music). It is not just the labor of the maroons but their prophetic organization that is negated by the idea of intellectual space in an organization called the university. This is why the negligence of the critical academic is always at the same time an assertion of bourgeois individualism.

Such negligence is the essence of professionalization where it turns out professionalization is not the opposite of negligence but its mode of politics in the United States. It takes the form of a choice that excludes the prophetic organization of the Undercommons to be against, to put into question the knowledge object, let us say in this case the university, not so much without touching its foundation, as without touching one's own condition of possibility, without admitting the Undercommons and being admitted to it.

University Experience:
Neoliberalism Against the Commons
Jason Read

As something of a hypothesis, I suggest that we view the question of the university through its tensions and contradictions. As several contributors to the discussions on Edu-factory have already indicated, these contradictions can be broadly categorized through the way in which the university is both a site of the commons, of the circulation of knowledge, and of neoliberal restructuring. Secondly, I think that these tensions can be viewed most productively as not just the tensions between different principles, the pursuit of knowledge versus the training of future employees, but between different practices, practices that ultimately produce different modes of living and thinking; that is, different formations of subjectivity.

To illustrate what I mean by the connection between practices and subjectivity, we can start with the image of the college student as rebel, and connect this to fundamental practices of college life. If for decades the figure of the student was synonymous with social rebellion, with a ruthless criticism of everything existing, this may have less to do with theories taught at the university, than with a particular practice, a particular experience of living. Universities uproot students from their homes, from their familiar and entrenched place in a familial order, and place them in a context that is halfway between communism (collective living, eating, sleeping) and anarchism (the necessity of creating a social order ex nihilo, even if it is only the social order of two, between roommates). On top of this there is all of the time, free from work and other demands; time to spend in clubs and social activities. There is something radical about student life, independent of the classroom, in the way in which it produces new experiences, and experiments in living. (Or at least there was, more on this below.) Moreover, we could add to this liminal experience of college life, the fact that the life of a student is an immersion in a particular form of intellectual commons. These commons take multiple forms, from the library with its often overlooked stacks of books, to the more flashy and visible forms of "information commons" and the access to high speed internet. (The latter has become one of the main perks of college life.) What links these different practices, different forms of the common together, is that in each case the common or collective use or appropriation of knowledge is seen as the necessary condition of any individual production, or use. Intellectual production, writing papers, doing experiments, etc., requires the collective and shared work of others. (I am indebted to George Caffentzis for this point). Thus, one side of student life is a veritable education in not only the commons, in the free and collective exchange of knowledge that is at the basis of every discovery, but in social experimentation and transformation. This side is countered by the neoliberal structuring of the university, a restructuring that is as much a matter of practices, modes of living and subjectivity, as it is of policy. The cut in funding to state universities and the rise of tuition have as their effects not only the shifting of the funding of education from a public good to a private good, but a transformation of how education is lived and experienced. Students at state universities work jobs, on campus and off, and are often forced to live at home. Thus, the liminal moment of the university, that made the subject position of the college student anomalous, neither child not adult, is being eradicated. College life is caught between the double pinchers of childhood and adulthood. The gap between these spaces is closed; one now answers to parents and to future employers at the same time. What we see in the university is a neoliberal production of subjectivity, a production that can be understood as a response to the liminal and collective production of subjectivity. As Michel Foucault argues in his lectures on neoliberalism, one of the central aspects of neoliberal theory and practice is the refiguring of human beings as "human capital." Everything that makes up the human individual, intelligence, appearance, education, marriage, location, can be understood as an investment of time or energy that makes possible future earnings. As Foucault writes: "Homo economicus is an entrepreneur and an entrepreneur of him or herself" (Michel Foucault, *Naissance de la biopolitique: Cours au Collège de France, 1978–1979*, Paris: Seuil: Gallimard, 2004, 239). As much as the university is an experience underwritten by the commons, by collective use and sharing of knowledge, it is interpreted, especially by those who attend it, as an investment in their human capital. Every class, every extracurricular activity, every activity or club becomes a possible line on a resume, becomes an investment in human capital. The question asked by every student at practically every college or university is: "how will this help me get a job?" This interpretation of the university experience is not just a product of a prevailing neoliberal ideology, but is actively produced by the overwhelming feeling of insecurity and fear that is brought about by the cuts in university funding. The partisans of the "Culture Wars" are correct to see the university as a struggle over hearts and minds, but incorrect in where they locate this struggle. It is not so much a matter of content, of Smith versus Marx or the western canon versus its many others, but of the form of knowledge itself. Is knowledge a social good, a common, which must circulate in order to produce effects? Or is it a commodity, something that can be purchased, an investment that has value only as property? These conflicting understandings of the value of knowledge are conflicts that are embodied in the practices of the university, in its structure. As such they have the potential to extend beyond the ivory towers of the university, to spill over into two very different understandings of the organization of society: one based on the commodity, on private possession of knowledge, resources, and rights, the other based on the commons. (On this point see Nick Dyer-Witheford, "The Circulation of the Common" http://www.geocities.com/immateri-allabor/withefordpaper2006.html.) The political question then is how to develop the commons against their neoliberal reduction to property and investments? To subjectivize the commons, making them a way of life?

The Autonomous University and the Production of the Commons, or, "Pirates were Resourceful, like Ninjas, they Learned to Use their Environments"

James Arvanitakis

One day at the university in which I lecture — University of Western Sydney — a student ran into me in the corridor. He said that he wanted to remind me that it was "international speak like a pirate day," and I should announce it in the lecture. As we walked and discussed the likely history of such a day, he noted that I, like many famous pirates, had learnt to adapt to my new environment: away from the more prestigious "sand stone" universities to one established to serve the lower-socioeconomic areas of greater Western Sydney, I was changing my language to suit the new students I was meeting. As I thanked him and headed for my second cup of coffee, he turned and said: "James... pirates were resourceful, like ninjas, they learnt to use their environment."

What do pirates and ninjas have to do with any proposed autonomous university? Maybe I will come back to that a little later but this scheduled post will be focussed on my autonomous education initiatives, which I have tried to adapt to my environment.

The debate so far: different pirates, different flags

I have followed the debate so far on the Edu-factory list serve. I am a fan of open source software, so I liked those entries. I am also, however, sceptical of its many claims, so have also liked those posts. What we can or cannot learn from open source is one way to see a key division within this list serve.

The second area is to discuss hierarchies and how they work. I feel comfortable with some hierarchies — thanks Ben and Avinash: I like having mentors at the university who I can look to for advice and learn from. I also accept that there are different hierarchies in knowledge; I know a lot more about the race theory than my students. Though I have experienced racism — particularly when I was younger — I give in to this hierarchy of knowledge when my black-Muslim student who has experienced racism in this country talks of someone trying to rip off her headscarf.

Saying that, however, there are other hierarchies with which I am uncomfortable . There are some fields of knowledge that claim authenticity or argue that they are more scientific than others. I still read student honor's level projects that have an implicit apologetic tone if they have not used enough quantitative research: an apology encouraged by their supervisors.

Only recently a PhD student was told to keep his personal feelings out of a thesis even though he had personal experience in the area he was writing: being removed from his parents because of his Aboriginality.

It is negotiated hierarchies that I am comfortable with.

Education as commons: staking my claim/ raising my flag

My position is reflected in the third theme that has arisen, and that education should be seen as a commons (as noted in the post by Jason Read). The commons can confront scarcity and create abundance.

Here I am talking about the commons in the "cultural" sphere. I argue that the commons can include human relationships such as the need for safety, trust, shared intellect, as well as simply cooperation. Briefly focusing on "safety," for example, I would argue that safety as a commons can be understood as both a sense of peace and an absence of fear. It can be thought of as mediated by a sense of belonging that allows members of communities to interact with each other. Cultural commons such as safety represent a form of biopolitics that promotes the potential for greater cooperation. That is, if I feel safe within my community, even when surrounded by strangers, then I am likely to cooperate with them. Safety can produce relationships that are non-hierarchical and inclusive, allowing communities to work together to overcome scarcity, crisis and fear (Hardt and Negri 2004, *Multitude*, xvi).

I see education as a cultural commons: something that we all share and can grow to expand creating a new form of biopolitical production. To do this, where possible, I make my research and own intellectual work available for all. I only expect that those who use it do the same for me in return — even if this is simply feedback: as one student once said: "dude, that really sucked, made no sense at all."

Only by openly sharing can our intellect and education really grow. But this too must be negotiated: I would refuse to allow my work around, say "understanding trade" to be available to a right wing racist group. I also respect that some people do not like politics.

This negotiation is different from enclosure — the commodification and patenting of knowledge that most universities now encourage through a variety of mechanisms. That is, the fact that we are often required to sell off our research to a "corporate partner" or that the university patents research to sell off at some future time. This is enclosure that promotes a scarcity in knowledge — and as any economist will tell you, the scarcer something is, the more value it has. Such scarcity has important implications for education and intellect.

My initiatives: the pirate (or ninja) in me

My initiative is simple: I believe in the democratization of knowledge and therefore do my best to distribute the education material that I have produced in different formats that are accessible to all. One way that I have done this is through MySpace (http://profile.myspace.com/index.cfm?fuseaction=user.viewprofile&friendid=127104278) blog-site.

Yes, I know, big bad Rupert Murdoch owns MySpace — but, like open source software, if we can use these tools as mechanisms for an autonomous university initiative, then why not? And, more importantly, these tools are used by many of my students. If this is a way I can discuss Marx, Foucault, Weber, Hardt and Negri with them, then this is the tool I will use. I use other mechanisms too, but MySpace is the one that has proven incredibly popular. Here students interact with me on their own terms.

(Another mechanism is a scotch and coffee get together we organize — but as it is 9 in the morning here, I will not get into that.)

It is this way, by making the information accessible—both in the way it is discussed and available — that I believe that we can find some insights into autonomous university knowledge production.

This way, autonomous universities can exist both inside and outside institutions, be simultaneously local and global and be available to all.

My vision: the treasure

I would love to establish a network of practitioners who work on such initiatives and who openly share our knowledge, information and work — agreeing that we all have different methods. I would also love to have a physical site somewhere: to got to and learn and teach, where others can do the same and to share: be they established theorists or activists looking to discuss their experiences.

From a Liberal Arts Student
Erik Forman

I was excited to hear about the experiments in Italy and Argentina, as they are very similar to what we are doing at my college. I also wanted to chime in to put my own perspective out there as a student at a (self-proclaimed) "elite" US liberal arts college — by definition a rare position to be in.

In the discourse of neoliberalism, liberal arts colleges are often looked upon as the "last bastion" of substantive education in an increasingly instrumentalized global "Edu-factory." I would like to interrogate this view of the liberal arts by looking critically at recent events at my own college, and poking tentatively toward a notion of education truly in opposition to neocolonialism and neoliberalism. At the end I will also describe a few of the projects students have initiated on my campus in reaction to the moves of the college administration toward greater elitism and exclusion.

Class Repolarization and the Liberal Arts

Education has long occupied a special place in the mythology of the US middle class. In the post-war era, access to education was seen as a hallmark of the classless society that was the American Dream. By selling education as a ticket out of the working class, capital effectively harnessed the power of exodus to reproduce class society. But if Keynesian economic systems prided themselves on the number of students they produced, neoliberalism has reversed this by turning exclusion itself into a measure of "excellence." My college is a textbook example of this transition.

In the mid-1990s the college I attend was given a huge philanthropic gift by the publisher of Readers' Digest (one of the hallmark "successes" of capitalist globalization). This money was used to transform a good regional college into a powerhouse of "academic excellence" and "global citizenship." With new resources at its fingertips, the college embarked on an ambitious plan to scale the heights of the *US News and World Report* rankings (this is a major capitalist news magazine in the US that publishes a popular college ranking guide). This scale has redefined the college's development plans far into the future. The distribution of resources on campus has been shifted away from financial aid, and toward programs embracing the rhetoric of "academic excellence" and "global citizenship." Private colleges have always served an elite, but rarely I think has the culture of these places been so blatantly supportive of class hierarchy. There isn't even a pretense to "accessibility" any more. Evidently, "global citizenship" isn't for everyone.

The transformation has manifested itself most baldly in the college's marketing efforts to attract more of a specific kind of applicants. The college markets itself (look at the website http://www.macalester.edu) as that most precious commodity on the market today — a community. College has become a place people flock to and then flee. It is the "place of refuge" in postmodern culture, the simulacrum of community. People hate being there, but most people stay. All the students are stressed out, many are worried about grad school and their careers, and many others feel immobilized to fight the system by the "privilege" they have been given. Some students certainly thrive on self-exploitation, and become successful yuppies. But it is recognized by most students on the left that we will end up working for nonprofits doing things we don't believe in, or will go to grad school for lack of a better idea. We feel condemned to become a sick appendage of a class we want no part of. A malaise hangs over the student body; everyone is always on the brink of dropping out, but few have the courage.

Maybe because of this, campus dissidents have until recently taken a purely conservative stand against the overt use of our campus as a training camp for global elites. This has created phenomenal tensions, with several students expelled for politically-motivated vandalism. In 2004, my first year on campus, the Board of Trustees proclaimed a "financial crisis" (sound familiar?) and voted to begin considering the ability of students to pay tuition as a criteria for admission (called "Need-Aware"). Tuition is now over $40,000 per year. Students and a small group of faculty and alumni mounted a campaign to "Defend Need-Blind Admissions at Macalester." We lost when they held the vote over Winter break. About 200 students (1/9th of the school) walked out of class early in the Spring semester, but didn't take over any buildings. On some level we accepted the legitimacy of their decision and did not feel that we could reverse it. Because the discourse of "excellence" has legitimacy, we felt that the college would have no trouble branding us as irrational and bringing in the cops to beat us down.

EXCO and Tent State

A bunch of other projects gained impetus from this failure, none of which have yet actually been able to build political power to change the college's agenda. In Spring 2006 students began planning to set up an Experimental College, a system through which anyone and everyone can teach or take a class for free. We were inspired by similar projects that came into existence around 1970 all over the US.

EXCO (http://www.excotc.org) came to fruition in Fall 2006. Classes on everything from Anarchism to the History of New York are now being attended by over 100 people. After flirting with campaigning for official course credit from my college for participation, EXCO is now attempting instead to generalize itself in the Twin Cities, escaping the student ghetto it was founded in. We hold classes all over the city, and are seeking to foster more community involvement. Of course, this involves running into the reality of class privilege which allows some people to attend EXCO classes, and not others, so our alternative needs to be connected to a political project to gain space in which most people can organize their own lives and educations. We return to the class basis of liberal education, and return to anticapitalist politics. That's where our latest project comes in.

From an EXCO class on Anarchist Anthropology last fall, a small group formed which began planning a mobilization for this Spring called "Tent State." This is basically a more oppositional form of EXCO. We are occupying the "Commons" (ha ha) of our campus as well as two other colleges in the area next week to offer teach-ins and hold discussions on themes affecting students. We are networked with Tent States across the US (and one in the UK!). You can look at our website here: http://www.tentstatemn.org. We want to be expansive, creating encounters between people who wouldn't normally meet.

I hope that this begins to form a new student subjectivity, one which actually transcends the limitations of the liberal arts campus and reflects the transformations of higher education over the last forty years that have destroyed the base of student movements in the US. I want to help build a new student body, a cyborg perhaps, that is inclusive of all those who learn for their entire lives to keep themselves on the market. We need to build solidarity across all the layers of exclusion that stratify the working class. I think that this is very similar to the idea of multitude if we think of this concept as building a heterogeneous political body to surpass the transformations of the technical composition of the working class wrought by capital after the movements of the 1960s and 1970s. For this, I think we need some new kind of student syndicate organization. This will be a challenging task.

What common threads emerge in all this?

In all our projects at my college (and now in our city), we are seeking to basically steal as much as possible from the university (thank you Brian Holmes for this awesome concept), while using the space and resources as a launching pad to construct our own alternatives with our own values, with as many different kinds of people as possible. In a limited sense we are rejecting the best that capitalism has to offer: the liberal arts. Admittedly, almost everyone keeps one foot in the rat race, but with the other we seek a path out of the enclosures of capital. Instead of a degree that grants "success" and in doing so perpetuates class society, we want an autonomously self-directed education that produces incommensurable subjectivities and allows us to send the arc of our own life trajectories beyond the options granted by the market.

I could go on and on about how EXCO and Tent State don't quite fill this role, and what we are thinking about doing to change this (better anti-racist work and more explicit anti-capitalism are two ideas), but this chapter is already long enough. I just wanted everyone to know that even at elite liberal arts colleges in the belly of the beast, there are those who would rather get the hell out than sell out. As long as we can pay off our loans.

Conflicts in the Production of Knowledge
Universidad Experimental

An introduction

There are invitations to which we are indifferent. We forget them immediately. There are, however, invitations that remain. They float in our heads, intertwining with other ideas. When the invitation is to a group, the idea no longer floats in one head but in several. Remaining open to these other heads, it is available to be taken and processed. The invitation to the debate about conflicts in the production of knowledge has affected us in this second way. For us, it is literally a vital problem.

We have tried, then, to think about this problem from our experiences as a group. That is to say, we have tried to list the conflicts that are taking places as our project moves. In schematic form, we have classified these conflicts under three categories:

- ➤ our relations with the logic of the State University;
- ➤ our relations with the logic of the Market University;
- ➤ the relations we maintain with our project insofar as it attempts a different kind of instituent wager with respect to knowledge and thought;

In this sense, we tried to turn this analytic into a strategic tool — a resource for the project. At the same time, we do not cease to question, modify or revise this analytic. For that reason, this text is only a small part of our discussion.

On the other hand, you will notice that this text lacks some kind of testimonial or chronicle of the experiences of the Experimental University throughout 2006. It seems to us much more stimulating to offer certain theses on the initial debate that also provide a kind of elaboration of what actually happened.

The Experimental University and the State University: conflicts

The Experimental University neither remains indifferent to nor exclusively confronts the State University, since it inhabits another logic. Its gesture is not so much exodus as camping. This response, before being an ideological question, concerns a specific availability of resources.

The hypothesis of the *piqueteros*, although not in all its aspects, helps to show the relationship we have with the State University: we do not want to fight over academic positions; we do not want to take over the student center. We want resources for the self-management of our projects. The university can digest the works of any thinker but it seems much more difficult for it to digest participatory forms of debate and construction. It seems, then, that with the State University, we can develop "contact surfaces" with regard to reading/writing/interventions but not with regard to management. It cost us highly at the singular and the collective level to find usable resources for our project in the State University, but in the meantime we were playing and hitting up against the institution all the time. Our wager is to subtract a fragment of the social interchanges of the university from state and market regulations in order to compose them with other social processes for the production and organization of life.

The Experimental University and the Market University: conflicts

Since in the mercantile era that which does not self-manage is either dismissed or absorbed by the market, our objective is to plot a "contract/contact" with the participants of the Experimental University that goes beyond this mercantile absorption. To insist on the "contract" with the different people involved in this experience is to make clear that our wager is a political wager. Our wager is to work as a connective machine between those involved in the Experimental University and processes of social self-organization.

If we bet on participatory action, then our wager serves as a platform of connections with different points of productive self-organization, which will necessarily lead us to redesign the processes of self-education. The Experimental University and the Market University generate two parallel poles of management of the State University's resources. Therefore, the conflict with the Market University does not appear as much in the subtraction of resources as it does within the interior spaces of the Experimental University itself. The whole strategy of the Experimental University, then, depends on the subjectivity that inhabits it. The subjectivity that produces the Market University is that of the consuming student. If one tries to break with the mercantile ways of life that we inhabit, the possibility emerges for new kinds of relations.

The Experimental University: conflicts

Our project positions us in the middle of a conflict between old and new organizational configurations that have as their agglutinative element the production of knowledge and its relation to other social spaces. What is at stake is the political productivity of knowledge and thought, which we have taken as a criterion that allows us to elaborate strategies. There does not exist a privileged space for the practices of the Experimental University, but nor does it have a privileged practice. Its importance lies in its political productivity for the construction and support of spaces in which it is possible to decide on all the dimensions we consider relevant to our existence. The Experimental University attempts to function as an attentive, moving and connective space, not as an auto-referential one. A double cognitive movement seems to install itself in our project: we seek, on the one hand, to invent a defining characteristic, a signature; and at the same time, to approach thinking no longer thematically but problematically.

We thus say it is not only a matter of instrumentalizing concepts in relation to problems, but also of not ceasing to question and redefine this same logic of instrumentalization. We try to conceptualize knowledge only insofar as it can serve as a tool with which to think and intervene in our realities. The fact that this form of knowledge can come into being in infinite ways, gives us the possibility to think that any kind of group can innovate constantly in its practice. Language itself is thought as a material that has in its immanence the power of being connective — that is, to assemble itself in unusual ways. On the basis of these connections, new forms of movement can be developed, both in thought and praxis, which are not within the repertoire of the quotidian.

If the traditional free universities (*cátedras libres**) generate hierarchical divisions between those who know and those who do not know, between experimental and non-experimental militants, the Experimental University sustains itself on another premise: "All of us involved in the project are the possessors of problems, that is to say, we ourselves become permanently problems." Today we consider that the dispute within, against and beyond the university must acquire a profile that privileges cognitive, methodological and connective aspects.

Can an institution that produces knowledge be defined exclusively by this triad? Absolutely not. Those are its defining traits, but not its only ones. The institution is also management, that is, the ways of managing of these elements.

* *"Cátedras libres"* (free universities) are open academic spaces usually created by militant student groups and organized in the traditional way: active teachers, passive students, etc.

Management conditions the logics of knowledge production from the inside. Command is not purely exterior with regard to the products: the historicity of these products is integrated in their very constitution.

What did we mean when we spoke about the "resources of the university?" Since one of our characteristics is precisely to inquire into the nature of our own collectivity (the very possibility for its existence, as much as the conditions it suffers and the profiles it adopts), we know that "a resource is never only a resource." To put it colloquially: the essence of any resource is to be a poisoned gift. This ambivalence leads us to a permanent interrogation of the political utility of resources.

The Global Autonomous University
Vidya Ashram

Knowledge Against Society

The twentieth century has been a century of knowledge production. It has also been a century of unprecedented violence. The knowledge that we produce is eventually turned against ourselves and against the whole of society. While this was also true of the modern university, knowledge society that is in the making now seems to be singularly designed to appropriate knowledge and turn it against the producers of knowledge in the service of global capital and global machineries of violence.

The university in the modern era was the prime location of knowledge production, which claimed to take society out of the darkness of ignorance into enlightenment and from a regime of scarcity to a condition of abundance. While the university did produce a great deal of knowledge the motion of this knowledge was such that it ended up being a handmaiden of profit and domination. On account of its sole authority in knowledge production, the university became complicit in suppression of society's knowledge. The bargain that the university made offered a space of pure enquiry, of knowledge for knowledge's sake, of pursuit of knowledge without interference from power. The university defended this privilege as much as it could. Now this privilege is being withdrawn.

The university has undergone major transformations in the twentieth century. A massive expansion of the university has been going on. Millions have access to higher education. Protocols of knowledge production in the university have been challenged from various directions. Women, blacks, erstwhile colonized, workers, rebels — all have challenged the higher education scenario in the world. But along with these processes of democratization of knowledge, a parallel movement of militarization and industrial-ization of knowledge production was ushered in with the Manhattan project. These two processes, of democratization and militarization/industrialization, seem to have come to a head in the 1960s, which saw numerous student ac-tions on campuses across the world.

Now the global order is reinventing itself. In the information age, there is not going to be a privileged set of knowledge producers who will be allowed an autonomous space, a safe haven to explore and invent. Knowledge will be harnessed from the whole cultural field and subjected to regimes of cognitive measurement, knowledge management, and information enclosures.

Hierarchies of Knowledge and Labor

Exploitation of labor was the hallmark of industrial society. Exploitation of knowledge is now being added to exploitation of labor to build the foundations of a new capitalist system. Knowledge from all locations — university, Inter-net, religions, ordinary life — are sought to be harnessed and exploited in the service of the building of this "knowledge society." Technologies of virtuality play an essential role in this management of knowledge. Living knowledge and its exploitation is an essential ingredient of the new production systems unlike the earlier systems, which depended on knowledge embodied in machines and routines. These developments open the way for a self-awareness of workers as bearers and producers of knowledge. There is no contradiction between knowl-edge and labor, nor is there a gulf between "knowledgeable bodies" and "la-boring bodies." Such contradictions stem from the division between mental and physical labor — a relic of the earlier industrial civilization. However, it is now perhaps the time to foreground the human being as an epistemic being.

The category of labor as it was constituted in the older capitalist system and as deployed even by socialist and communist ideologies of workers' emancipation implies a hierarchy of labor in society — intellectual labor, in-dustrial labor, women's labor, artisanal labor, agricultural labor, primitive labor, the idler and so on. It seems to us that this labor hierarchy is implic-itly constructed on the basis of the knowledge hierarchy among the various kinds of knowledge that exist in society. University knowledge and modern science and technology occupied the space of knowledge while womens' knowledge, farmers' knowledge, artisanal knowledge, tribal knowledge were considered a product of habit or accident, if not expressions of pure su-perstition. We reject such descriptions and the resulting hierarchy. Even in the modern era, such knowledge in society that we call *lokvidya* has played an important role in the survival of the people whose knowledge traditions these constitute.

If we grant that there is no hierarchy among various locations of knowledge in society and that all kinds of knowledge have a role to play in the reconstruction of society, the grounds for non-hierarchical solidarities across many boundaries is prepared. Moreover, epistemic recognition of lokvidya opens us to a vast realm of living knowledge traditions in society as forms of autonomous knowledge activity. This also creates the condition for people to see their own knowledge traditions as sources of strength, and not only as means of survival.

Unlike the industrial society, the knowledge society does recognize lokvidya. But lokvidya is recognized only in order to economically benefit from it. In fact, the relation that knowledge society constructs with any knowledge is essentially one of economic exploitation. Knowledge society is built on the integration of any knowledge by economic exploitation.

Autonomous Global University (AGU)

The Edu-factory Collective's proposal of the formation of AGU is a bold idea. It has the potential to project a transformative perspective on knowledge society. We support its formation.

To say that AGU is autonomous is to say that the knowledge activity of such a university is free from political interference, economic pressures and military requirements. This requires that it has a political and ideological significance of its own.

Autonomy in the context of knowledge in this age of corporatization means above all the regulation of knowledge activities by epistemic norms derived from knowledge activity outside the market. Knowledge activity outside the market relates to a large part of knowledge in society, lokvidya and various cultural, political and other expressions and representations which are consciously kept autonomous.

Autonomous Global University (AGU) is not just another site of knowledge production. It is a site of cooperation among knowledge producers and a site of non-cooperation with the global regime of knowledge. It is a university in so far as its stock activity is knowledge activity. We can perhaps think of it as a union of networks and organizations. Of necessity, it will operate mainly through the virtual realm. But it is composed of acts of resistance and acts of organization on the ground.

AGU values all kinds of labor and all kinds of knowledge equally. AGU looks at knowledge as a means of reconstruction of society and individuals. AGU looks at knowledge as means of liberation, livelihood, culture. AGU thus works for the recognition and representation of all forms of knowledge in society. AGU seeks to step out on the periphery of time and gaze into the future;

it seeks to build an imagination of the future society which is not just a variant of global capitalism. Through its activities it seeks to create idioms of global emancipatory transformations.

AGU looks at why our knowledge is turned against ourselves. It seeks to build solidarities across borders of the university and within the universities, solidarity of all bearers and producers of knowledge. It is not a bastion of creativity and production. It is an organ of dialogue, solidarity and organization. It seeks to organize the relatively empowered section of knowledge producers which are located in the university in order to challenge the global mechanisms of exploitation and violence. It seeks to expose the ways and means by which knowledge becomes an instrument of profit and a weapon against society. AGU seeks to emancipate knowledge from this condition.

For this purpose, AGU seeks to spread the virus of non-cooperation to all universities. We have read about the various auto-education initiatives in the earlier round of discussion — in Argentina, Europe, US, India — and about movements of students and precarious workers in Greece and other places. The various auto-education initiatives and movements at the borders of the university and within it can be read as acts of non-cooperation with the institutionalization of a new order of knowledge. This new order of knowledge exploits students, teachers and their knowledge for profit and control. These acts resist the enfeeblement and enslavement of knowledge producers and seek to liberate knowledge from the clutches of dons, managers, and rent seekers.

AGU seeks to link these acts of non-cooperation to create forums and launch activities that direct an uncompromising light on the prevailing order of things. By being a site of dialogues and translations, AGU seeks to sow the seeds of a social movement of knowledge, a *knowledge satyagraha*. Knowledge satyagraha means the insistence that knowledge activities be regulated by epistemic norms independent of the market, the insistence that knowledge be linked to values of truth and justice. "Non-cooperation" and "satyagraha" as forms of political action are legacies most notably of the non-violent mass movement against the British Empire during the Indian freedom struggle and the civil rights movement in the US.

AGU seeks to participate in a reconstruction of knowledge and initiate a reconstitution of university. It explores ways and means of building and instituting a new imagination of university that operates in an environment of knowledge abundance. It seeks to reinterpret and reorganize the vast amounts of knowledge that have been generated by the university so far. It challenges the prevailing institutionalized differentiations of knowledge like the one between the sciences and arts. It seeks to reinterpret human sciences by inscribing human being as an epistemic being at its core. It seeks to develop new principles of integration of knowledge.

We understand that the challenge of actualizing a vision like this is immense. All the tools available in the virtual realm — website, mailing list, wiki, blogs, social networking — will have to be configured and reconfigured. The relation between the virtual life and the ordinary life will also have to be reflected upon, since we are seeking to connect the two. The new institutional form of AGU will have to be elaborated further and its relation with other institutional forms defined. Since this is the first time we are discussing the construction of an autonomous global university, we felt we will try to articulate a possible vision for AGU, rather than try to work out all aspects of it.

Lokvidya And AGU

From the point of view of relationship with the market lokvidya activity may be divided into three parts:

First, lokvidya which has been coopted by the global market often through the new techniques brought into existence by the Internet. Secondly, lokvidya activity that operates on the margins of the market. This however contributes greatly to the creation of riches by its numbers and vastness. Household production of all types based both on artisanry and farming belong to this category. Thirdly, those lokvidya processes that have no immediate economic value attached to them and are therefore outside the market.

Globalization has tried to construct trade routes and linkages for an economic exploitation of all such activity but what gets left out still constitutes large part of social reality, at least in countries like India. A lot of work at home and in remote geographical areas is of this type. Womens' work in the house which includes bringing up children, daily health care, balanced food, cooking, sanitation and cleanliness, decoration etc. is work of this type which is definitely based on a steady understanding and knowledge of human beings and their surroundings. To this category also belongs a large part of the activity of tribals and indigenous people in remote areas. They grow food on small plots of land to eat, make and repair implements of their use, build houses, and collect forest produce as food, medicine and fuel. Their life is split into two parts, one constituted by all of these knowledge-based activities outside the market and other of work in the market as workers for wages. Similarly, almost all households, including often the very organized urban households too, have these two components, one of women's work outside the market and the other of men and women earning through the market.

So there is this huge expanse of activities of women and tribals and part of the activity of peasants and artisans, which is outside the market and is based on their knowledge that is modified and upgraded regularly and is full of innovations. We would like to further explore, and would like to invite others to explore, what relevance this aspect of lokvidya can have in constructing an epistemic frame of reference which may provide the guidelines for knowledge activity of an autonomous university.

Vidya Ashram

We end with a brief introduction to some activities and plans of Vidya Ashram which bear an affinity with the initiative for the construction of an autonomous global university. Vidya Ashram (www.vidyaashram.org) was set up three years ago at Sarnath near Varanasi. Sarnath is the place where Buddha first expounded his philosophy of becoming.

Among other activities, we have organized a series of dialogues on Knowledge in Society in various fora associated with World Social Forum process during the last four years. The dialogues were held at Hyderabad, Mumbai, Karachi, Delhi. We intend to take these dialogues to universities, among computer professionals and generally among people. We hope that these dialogues will lead to the formation of a new academy. This academy, which might possibly be named the Lokvidya Academy, will seek to reconfigure relations between different kinds of knowledge in society and between knowledge and society.

Last year Vidya Ashram formed an Emancipation of Knowledge Forum. A group of 30 young men and women from the Sarnath region have joined to shape this forum. Attempts to extend it around Varanasi are going on. We hope that this forum can develop as a platform for various organizations and movements to come together to explore the political significance of the knowledge question which might lead to new radical forms of politics.

APPENDICES

On the Institution of the Common

Toni Negri and Judith Revel

1 We would like to begin by reporting a recent reflection on the definition of "autonomous workers' institution" (AWI) — a definition which we have discussed in trying to develop a historiographic outline of the institutionality of the workers' committees in Porto Marghera and their activities in the late 1960s and 1970s. By AWI, on that occasion, we meant an organization characterized by

(a) an independent capacity to put forward themes of struggle, together with the consequent and coordinated indication of instrumental actions, therefore possessing its own normative capacity;

(b) an autonomous capacity to organize and conduct political and wage struggles in significant industrial and/or social sectors and, therefore, an autonomous capacity to exercise the legal strength in support of the organized action;

(c) the actual recognition by other institutions (trade-unions, political institutions, workers, bosses) co-existing in the same industrial and/or social sectors, and, therefore, a certain social legitimization of its normative capacity and use of force.

Should we wish to deepen this definition, we could emphasize that the normative capacity of the AWI is formed through processes of self-learning, moving from the bottom to the top, from a political and technological experience to an alternative conceptualization and planning, from linguistic production to the construction of one (or multiple) appropriate praxis. When we speak of the normative capacity of the AWI, we refer to a collective intelligence. This is already implicit in self-formation processes, that take "con-research" as the basis for the construction of common concepts that can be transformed into means of action.

As for the political legitimacy of AWI, on one side it asserts itself as an instituent capacity (that is reflexive, tendentially normative), on the other — from the political viewpoint — it asserts itself as a constituent power and it can be developed into a political subject. Both the law and the sociology of labor (from Sinzheimer to Eugen Ehrlich, not to mention the theory of the Soviets, especially in their Luxembourghist version) have shown, for more than a century, the productivity of these definitions.

2. What does the AWI become in the transition to a new mode of production? What does it becomes in the passage from Fordism to post-Fordism? It should become an institution far more common than what it was in the previous mode of production, because the form of production has also become more common. We hypothesize, then, a new institution: a common autonomous institution (CAI) or a multitudinarian autonomous organization.

First, this new institution is founded on the new relational horizon (communicative, informatic etc.) that is characteristic of the new mode of production. This horizontal dimension is further characterized by its network form. Thus the net becomes the basis of the new common institution. Within this transition and this new formation, it is not easy (it is, in fact, impossible) to recognize autonomous characteristics in the sense indicated above. The CAI can begin to be defined as a "reticular institution," expansive but also dissipating, insofar as it considers itself and /or is recognized as a "nomadic" ("esodante") institution (where, however, this last determination is viewed only from an intensive viewpoint). That said, it is fully evident that this first element of institutionality (networked, "nomadic") lacks any specifically normative connotation. This means that what is lacking is any element that may enable us to insist (beside the horizontal definition) on a vertical transition, instituted on the basis of an autonomous organizational capacity and the actual recognition by other institutions and therefore the power of self-legitimization.

3. We propose a scholastic hypothesis. Any form of institution and/or government (from the most concentrated to the most diffused), is based upon power relations that develop genealogically on a horizontal dimension to then find themselves again in a vertical relation. We could add that every definition of IP is given as a point of equilibrum on an orthogonal screen, that includes on the ordinate the horizontal element, and on the abscissa the vertical element, that is the reticular consensus and the normative force, the assent to the structure and the exercise of command.

In the scheme previously defined, the public appears as a moment of equilibrium between the reticular complex of singularities reduced to the epistemic unit on the axis of the ordinate and the concentration of force established on the vertical axis. Now, this definition of IP is not satisfying from the viewpoint of the CAI: it does not manage to comprehend the expansive moment of the network. It grasps, as we said, the exodus only in its intensive dimension (see, on this point, the "weak" interpretations of the thought of Deleuze). Secondly, this definition cannot transfer the expansive power of the singularity from the forms to the forces, from episteme to ontology, it is not able then to form the force.

Let's conclude then: all this occurs because that reasoning — and that reality — is not able to descend from the forms to the forces. But even this is a fiction. In reality, within this crisis, we always imagine something that does not exist. This something is the public: the public does not exists, because the definition of the public is nothing other than the mystification of the common.

4. Let's try to verify this assertion. Let's start from the fact that that from the viewpoint of what we are used to call "the technical composition" of labor-power, production has become common. From the viewpoint of the "political composition," new juridical and political categories should correspond to this common composition, capable of organizing this "common," of expressing its centrality, describing its institutional figures and its internal functioning. Now these new categories do not exist yet. But we miss them. The fact that we mask the new dimension of the common and continue to reason in obsolete terms — as if the general place of production were still and only the factory, or as if the network were nothing but a flat communication figure — the fact, therefore, that that we continue to proceed as if nothing had changed (concerning the technical composition of labor-power): this is what the worst mystification of power consists of.

The mystification rests, in particular, on the ideological re-proposal of two terms that function like baits and cages, fictions and illusions, but correspond, at the same time, to two ways of appropriating "the common of men." The first of these two terms is the resort to the category of the "private," the second is the resort to the category of the "public." In the first case, property (Rousseau dixit: "…and the first man who said 'this is mine'…") is an appropriation of the common by one alone, that is also an expropriation of all the others. Today, private property consists precisely in negating wo/men their common right to what only their cooperation is capable of producing.

The second category that concerns us is that of "the public." The good Rousseau, who was so hard on private property (making of it, with good reason, the source of all corruption and human suffering) thus breaks down. It is the problem of the social contract, the problem of modern democracy: given that private property generates inequality, how do we invent a political system where everything, while belonging to everybody, nevertheless does not belong to anyone? "…n'appartienne pourtant a personne…"

The trap closes on Jean-Jacques as it does, on the other side, on us . Here it is what the public is: it is what belongs to all, but to nobody, that is, i.e. what belongs to the State. And given that we too should be the State (but obviously we are not, above all when we cannot manage to arrive at the end of the month) it is necessary to invent something to sweeten the bitter pill of the theft of the common: making us believe that it represents us, and if it [the State] advocates rights on what we produce, it does so because that "us" (that which we actually are) is not what we produce in common, what we invent and organize as a common, but what allows us to exist. The common, the State tells us, does not belong to us, because we do not really create it: the common, is our soil, our foundation, what we have under our feet, our nature, our identity. And if this common does not really belong to us — to be is not to have — the State's theft of the common will not be called appropriation, expropriation, but economic management, delegation and political representation. CVD: the implacable beauty of political pragmatism, the transformation of what we are, and that is common, into nature and identity.

5. At this point we can reconnect with the formal of the Cartesian coordinates with which we opened our discussion: that formal must be unveiled.

a) First of all, that formal, as we have seen, is very real. That equilibrium point is a utopia of power, in the attempt to castrate the common, to reduce it to a system of privation, to a model of the private that is called the public. In this consists the reactionary flotsom nestled in democracy — the continuity of property and the rhetorical tradition of individualism, the (Bourdieuian) habitus in the master classes and the habit of banal life. Here also exists exception, not as mythology of an extreme, exasperated power, but as the expression of a power full, well nourished with all the juridical right and previous customs: extremism of the center (the nice industrial and military tools of Goering, rather than Hitler's folly). That equilibrium, then, is very real, and it is immediately hostile to us. In the same way as all the coordinates, more or less transcendental or religious, are our enemies, from ecclesiastic law to the quacquaraquá of the kathechon.

b) Secondly, that formal is in itself contradictory, because in order to prevent the network of relations from displacing its subversive and cooperative potential from the horizontal to the vertical level of power, it is forced to negate any possible translation and therefore any power of singularity. It is forced to negate, that is, not only the relational, cooperative element, but also that innovative that resides in the bio-political determination of the network. (Here we should open a discussion on the various lines of interpretation of Foucault's thought).

c) Consequently, nature and identity represent the mystification of the modern paradigm of power. To re-appropriate the common, we must first of all produce a drastic critique of it.

We are by no means part of it and we do not want to be part of it. "We" is not an essence, a "thing" of which it is necessary to declare that it is public. On the contrary, our common is not our foundation, but it is a production, an invention continually begun anew. "We" is the name of an horizon, the name of a becoming. The common is always ahead of us, a process. We are this common: to make, to produce, participate, to move, to divide, circulate, enrich, invent, re-launch, etc.

For almost three centuries we have thought democracy as a public administration of the public thing [res publica], that is, as the institutionalization of the appropriation of the common. Today, democracy cannot any longer be thought of except in radically different terms: as common management of the common. This management involves a redefinition of space: reticular (without limits — but this does not means without hierarchies and internal borders — to the point of becoming cosmo-political) and a redefinition of the temporality: constituent. It is not a question of defining a form of contract according to which everything, by belonging to everybody, does not belong to anybody. No, everything, being produced by all, belongs to all.

As is evident from what we have said, this "belonging to everybody" is a becoming. It is the same thing as the constitution of the institutions of the multitude, in their non-teleological dynamic (a finality constituted through means each time productive in a chaotic whole, cannot be defined teleological), but dys-topic.

6. We believe that, at this point, the coordinates reconnect in the body and power (as it happens even in Descartes and, above all, in the modal parallelism of Spinoza). In body and power: that is, in constituent power, in a mechanism of translations that expresses new meanings. (We call them constituent power and mechanism of translation — in the terms used by Sakai, Solomon, and Mezzadra, and that is a constitutive dynamics from the bottom of languages, of the multitudes, and the institutions.) For us it is enough now to establish this — the ontological and temporal pre-valence of a constitutive device that defines the foundation of any constructive process of the institution of the common.

No pre-figuration of the institutions of the common is possible if we do not recognize a constituent power in action. This opens the way for some other problems that cannot be underestimated, starting from that ontological and temporal prevalence that we have attributed to constituent power. In particular: constituent power is first of all a juridical category, that is, one of the powers trapped (and in ..... definitely excluded) by public law. How can it be recuperated? Naturally, historical analysis remains fundamental, and it shows us how constituent power, any time it is exploded, has had ontological effects. But we are not interested now in the courses critical of the history of right: we are interested in identifying the political devices, the latent and expressed intentionality of constituent power (as a machine that produces institutions), in the actual conjuncture and that is as a machine to be used for the construction of a common right against public right. Putting it in these terms, the question of the institutions of the common becomes that of the assertion of constituent power as a permanent internal source of the process of political-juridical constitution of society.

a)   Within this research, we must evaluate the relations that social movements impose on governments, the material determinations that the movements design in constitutional set ups. Constituent power as an internal source of public and constitutional right is above all evident in the new constitutions of Latin America: it designs new relations and new constitutional dynamics both in terms of government and of governance, re-activating in this manner the common right of the multitudes so far excluded from power and thereby transforming the entire fabric of the democratic constitution.

b) Within this research, we must also again analyze the temporalities that implicitly and explicitly connect the action of the movements to constitutional determinations. When we look at the new dynamics that tie multidudinarian forms and constitutional set ups, in the transition processes that take place in the new economic areas (China, India, Brazil), we must recognize that new institutional figures are born (in the post-colonial experiences) that cannot be reduced to the models of European modernity.

Let us be careful, however, these suggestions for research derive from the objective analysis of the chaotic situation in which public institutions in Europe and the United States find themselves today, that is, in the states of capitalist modernity. Anticipations, traces of constituent power are found in the crisis in which public institutions agitate. We can, in this respect, build case histories, concentrating on the highest points of critical analysis and self-criticism of the juridical sciences (Teubner and the new course of juridical institutionalism) and the social sciences (Boltanski and the new course of sociological institutionalism). We believe that, in order to reshape the theme and redefine an eventual ideal-type of the institutions of the common, it is necessary to re-open and reinvent the inquiry on the level of the new capitalistic constitution of the social. We need to take on this phase of inquiry:

1.   Cognitive capital as a characteristic of the process of valorization;
2.   The metropolis as the new localization of exploitation;
3.   Finance capital as the new figure of general capital, in other words, the new figure of the form of command. Christus-fiscus, this is truly a terrain of antagonistic inquiry (Cristus subprimes etc.)
4.   Borders, hierarchies, and fragmentations, as an analytic of the multitude (and eventually of war);
5.   The translation of struggles/institutions as a terrain of possible political dystopias;

The constituent inquiry can define the political method of critical analysis and militant insubordination in this phase. Here, we have a new orthogonal table (considering that it all takes place in the network, in any case) which will perhaps allows us to grasp the element of innovation among the hunches and differences that the network itself proposes. If the geometry of the multitude cannot be flattened into that of the network, the geometry of revolution will, howeveer, probably correspond to the geometry of the institutions of the common.

In any case, this is the road that the constituent inquiry must assume as a hypothesis.

The Corporate University and the Financial Crisis: What Is Going On?

Christopher Newfield and the Edu-factory Collective

Edu-factory Collective: In the US over the last two decades, scholars and politicians have strongly discussed the crisis of the university. You contribute to this debate by authoring papers and books; could you give us the coordinates of this dispute?

Christopher Newfield: The crisis of the university was first caused by conservative attacks on the democratization of society that the post-World War II university — especially the public university — was spreading in American society. These attacks focused on the university not only because it harbored centrist and leftwing ideas, but also because it produces the scientific and technological innovations on which the business system depends, and the trained cadres that run that system — the so-called "workforce of tomorrow" without which no Internet company or investment bank could function for a day. The Right recognized in the 1960s that the university was producing a mass middle class that was openly disputing the worldview of the Cold War economic and military elites who had kept a firm grip on US politics in the 1950s. The university seemed to be the wellspring of these troublesome people, who were protesting racial segregation, sympathizing with the victims of colonization, and marching against nuclear weapons and the Vietnam War. Unlike large corporations, national politics, law firms, white churches, and other pillars of the establishment, the university was instilling technical knowledge, political confidence, and economic entitlement not just into a controllable elite but into the 50-60% of the population that by the mid-1970s had spent at least some time in college.

One flank of the Right's attack was the "culture wars," endless and largely successful attempts to discredit civil rights and public services (signalled by popular terms such as "cultural of dependency," "welfare queens") and to discredit the new social knowledge emerging from universities ("political correctness," "multiculturalism"). The Right targeted any form of academic knowledge that had been enriched by contact with social movements. The second flank was the budget wars, in which higher education was praised as the key to a successful "knowledge economy," while at the same time being cut in terms of public support. The sector that was specially targeted was the public universities that taught 80% of American college students by 1995. The numbers are disturbing: an Urban Institute study showed that higher education's share of state appropriations nationwide fell from 6.7% to 4.5% in the last quarter of the 20th century, and a University of California report found that state support for each of its students has fallen about 40 percent in real dollars since 1990.

The money that was cut was devoted to general public higher education — the activities that brought learning, independence, personal development, and leadership abilities to ordinary students. These cuts did not affect elite private schools or federally funded research: the schools whose graduates run Wall Street and Washington were wealthier than ever. This wealth came in large part from their investments in hedge funds and other "structured investment vehicles" that have recently blown up, but which were allowing the endowments of Harvard, Stanford, and Princeton to grow between 15% and 30% a year for a number of years in a row. Similarly, federal granting agencies oriented more of their programs toward commercial results and doubled their funding in real dollars between 1990 and 2005: 70% of this money went directly to business and most of the rest to universities.

Edu-factory: Thus, the financialization of the university was allowable by the budget wars. Financialization was a process which affected both the private and public university although in a different way. Contemporary capitalism does not, in fact, save the university from the financialization process that was one of its features just before the current financial crisis. In this regard, what role will university will in the political and cultural growth of contemporary society?

C. N.: The cuts spared the corporate end of higher education while squeezing its mass base. The dominant result is that the multitude of newly minted graduates, with poorer skills, more debt, and less exposure to citizen-building fields (whose own confidence has been severely damaged), cannot expect to have democratic control of their society, but must aspire to slots that will be doled out according to the political and economic leaderships' interpretation of economic conditions.

This brings us to the current crisis. The most immediate result will be further cuts in public services, including public universities. Wealthy elite schools will also be hurt this time: Cornell University has already announced a hiring freeze as it calculates its endowment losses, and others will follow. Federal research will be hit, affecting the budgets of the big research universities. The US ran a very large federal deficit during the boom in order to fight the war in Iraq and cut taxes on capital returns. Governments will be under tremendous pressure to run their public sector on the cheap, and higher education will continue to decline.

In a sense the financial crisis is the final triumph of the Right's "squeeze doctrine." This was developed during the Reagan administration: use market deregulation and tax cuts for the rich to degrade public services, undermine popular support for them, and create deficits so large that the government will be forced to cut itself again. In the universities, the outcome has been a kind of financial neutron bomb. It has left the technological fields standing, while disabling the fields associated with independent cultural and political thought and with social development.

Edu-factory: One more aspect of the articulation between the financial crisis and the crisis of the university seems, for us, to be the student loans system. This system works as the socialization of the risk inside the corporate university. By means of the student loan system, students take on their own a part of the risk of the corporate university, paying in advance a part of their future wages (as it happens for the future contract in the stock market). In fact, they are going to pay their student loans for several years after the end of their education.

In this framework, we could think about the student loans system as a sort of financialization of welfare. This is an ambivalent process: on one hand there is the students' recourse to credit to secure their access to education, on the other hand there is finance which generates a perverse response to people's need to access education. The perverse action of finance is the reduction of the students' future wages by the debts they contract for education.

This opens up a process of profound disqualification of both the academic work and knowledge production. This process, inside academia, works by the *déclassement* of labor power, by a strong increase of precarious and contingent labor, as well as by the process of loss of political confidence you refer to.

C. N.: Two things are happening at once. The first is the general increase in post-graduate debt (Nellie Mae, the student-loan provider, "found that the average student-loan debt had more than doubled" between 1991 and 1997; in addition, "the average credit card debt for the class of 2002 was over $3000." In that year, "39 percent of students [were] graduating with 'unmanageable levels of student loan debt'." For African American and Hispanic students, the levels were 55 percent and 58 percent, respectively. A few years later, the actual average student loan debt level for the class of 2007 was nearly $21,900: $19,400 for borrowers at public universities and nearly $25,700 for borrowers at private colleges. To keep things at even this low level of control, four-fifths of all undergraduates work in college, one-third of them full-time, the other two-thirds an average of twenty-five hours a week). Students lose future wages and become more dependent on accepting any kind of work they can find, and more pliable in those jobs. Student debt hasn't yet created debt servitude, but it increases financial insecurity and most likely political docility. Second, student debt has intensified both class and race inequality in the US. Latinos and African Americans are more likely to have unacceptable levels of student debt and to default on their debt later, which can create havoc in their personal lives. A third result is that students of color are increasingly found in two-year and local four-year colleges, and not at the major research publics or elite privates where they might have an Obama-style career path into major leadership positions. In addition, four-year universities are increasingly affordable only for more affluent students, and one result is that nearly all of the gains in college participation of the past 30 years have gone to students from the top 25% of family incomes. Finally, student debt discourages entry into the public sector and public-service oriented jobs. If one leaves law school with $125,000 in loans, one is less inclined to work in poverty or discrimination law for non-profits that pay $55,000 a year when one can join a corporate firm at $150,000 to start, and pay off one's creditors.

Edu-factory: Do you think it is possible to overturn the political docility connected with the debt system and open up a battlefield in which to fight against both the crisis of the university and the financial crisis? In Italy the current students' struggles have a slogan: "We won't pay for your crisis." Do you think it is possible to build up a similar process in the US context?

C.N.: That is an excellent slogan: we need it in the US! Most students and faculty act as though the crisis came like an earthquake or a hurricane, and that it is the new reality that requires us to lower our expectations. This is wrong, but few students and faculty are as yet fighting back: Americans may be obsessed with money, but they generally don't know much about how it works.

We need a new democratization movement that sees the public university as a cornerstone. So far, the faculty is missing in action. They are divided between tenure-track and non-tenure track (the latter, "adjunct" faculty teach

40% of all courses in US universities with no security of employment, much lower wages, higher course loads, and lesser benefits). They are also divided between "star" faculty who have international reputations and outside job offers that they can use to increases their individual salaries and research resources, and "stalwarts" who spend most of their time teaching and doing service and who have no individual salary leverage. This mixed-up and split-up group has not sided with students in demanding proper resources for combining mass access with high quality. Many of us continue to work on this, but only work stoppages and large-scale threats (all faculty applying for jobs at other universities, etc.) will match the enormous pressure coming from politicians to save the money for banks.

Everyone knows that you can't have democracy without a free press, one that is intellectually and financially independent. You also can't have a democracy without a free university. A regrouped democracy movement should rest in part on a demand for universal higher education — egalitarian access to the best quality, with its mission defined by its participants.

The Edu-factory Collective (www.Edu-factory.org) was born within the networks of precarious workers and students struggles in the Italian university, and now it is becoming a collective. It includes: Marco Baravalle, Claudia Bernardi, Simone Capra, Anna Curcio, Alberto De Nicola, Paolo Do, Ludovica Fales, Gabriella Garcia, Andrea Ghelfi, Camillo Imperore, Federico Marini, Miguel Mellino, Brett Neilson, Gigi Roggero, Davide Sacco.

James Arvanitakis teaches at the School of Humanities and Languages at the University of Western Sydney (Australia). He member of The Commons Institute (www.mercury.org.au/tci%20home.htm) and author of *The Cultural Commons of Hope: The Attempt to Commodify the Final Frontier of the Human Experience* (VDM Verlag Dr. Mueller e.K., 2007).

Franco Barchiesi teaches in the African American and African Studies Department at Ohio State University. He is an activist in the global movement and scholar of the *labor movement* in Africa. He edited *Rethinking the Labour Movement in the 'New South Africa'* (Ashgate, 2003).

Amit Basole teaches in the Economy Department at University of Massachusetts. He is an activist at the Center for Popular Economics, and engaged in struggles against processes of water privatizing. He has published several essays and articles on sciences, knowledge, and on the critique of euro-centrism.

Marc Bousquet teaches at Santa Clara University. An activist and organizer in university workers' struggles, he co-founded *Workplace: A Journal for Academic Labor*. He is author of *How the University Works: Higher Education and the Low-Wage Nation* (New York University Press, 2008).

George Caffentzis teaches in the Philosophy Department at the University of Southern Maine. A scholar and activist, he is coordinator of the Committee for Academic Freedom in Africa and a member of Midnight Notes Collective. He was editor of *Midnight Oil: Work, Energy, War, 1973–1992* (Autonomedia, 1992) and *A Thousand Flowers: Social Struggles Against Structural Adjustment in African Universities* (Africa World Press, 2000).

Counter Cartographies Collective (3Cs) was founded in the fall 2005 at the University of North Carolina, Chapel Hill. Information about their political activity is available at www.countercartographies.org.

Dionisis is an activist in the student movement in Greece. He wrote a number of reports for the Edu-factory list in 2006–2007 and also during the riots in Greece of December 2008.

Silvia Federici taught at Hofstra University. She is a radical feminist and co-founder of the Committee for Academic Freedom in Africa and a member of Midnight Notes Collective. She is the author of *Caliban and the Witch: Women the Body and Primitive Accumulation* (Autonomedia, 2004).

Erik Forman is student at Macalester College and a member of Experimental College (www.excotc.org).

Stefano Harney is Chair of Global Learning and Reader in Strategy at the School of Business and Management, Queen Mary University of London. A militant scholar of the work of C. L. R James, he is author of *State Work: Public Administration and Mass Intellectuality* (Duke University Press, 2006).

Randy Martin is Chair of the Art and Public Policy Department at New York University. He is a member of the *Social Text* collective and co-founder of Faculty Democracy, the faculty organization that supported the graduate student strike at NYU in 2005. He is editor of *Chalk Lines: The Politics of Work in the Managed University* (Duke University Press, 2001) and author of *Empire of Indifference: American War and the Financial Logic of Risk Management* (Duke University Press, 2007).

Sandro Mezzadra teaches in the Department of Politica, Istituzioni e Storia at Università di Bologna (Italy). A scholar and activist, he is part of the Uninomade project and author of *Diritto di fuga. Migrazioni, cittadinanza, globalizzazione* (Ombre Corte, 2006) and *La condizione postcoloniale. Storia e politica nel presente globale* (Ombre Corte, 2008).

Toby Miller is Director of the program in Film and Visual Culture at University of California, Riverside. He is the author of many books and edited *Postmodern Subject* (The Johns Hopkins University Press, 1993) and *Cultural Citizenship: Cosmopolitanism, Consumerism, and Television in a Neoliberal Age* (Temple University Press, 2006).

Fred Moten teaches in the English Department at Duke University. A scholar of Black Studies, he is author of *In the Break: The Aesthetics of the Black Radical Tradition* (University of Minnesota Press, 2003).

Toni Negri taught at Università di Padova and Ecole Normale Supérieure de Paris. A philosopher and political activist, he recently founded the Uninomade project and the journal *Posse*. He is author of many books and co-author with Michael Hardt of *Empire: The New Order of Globalization* (Harvard 2000) and *Multitude: War and Democracy in the Age of Empire* (Penguin 2004).

Brett Neilson is Director of the Centre for Cultural Research, University of Western Sydney. He is author of *Free Trade in the Bermuda Triangle... and Other Tales of Counterglobalization* (University of Minnesota Press, 2004) and has published in venues such as *Variant, Mute, Posse, DeriveApprodi, Vacarme, Subtropen, Conflitti globali, Il Manifesto, Carta, Open, transversal* and *Framework*.

Christopher Newfield is a Professor in the English Department at the University of California, Santa Barbara. An activist and scholar, he works on education and the American university. He is author of *Unmaking the Public University: The Forty-Year Assault on the Middle Class* and *The Post-Industrial University: The Culture Wars and the Unmaking of the American Middle Class, 1980–2005*.

Aihwa Ong teaches in the Department of Antropology at University of California, Berkeley. She works on diasporas, flexible citizenship and governmentality in Asia. Her most recent book is *Neoliberalism as Exception: Mutations in Citizenship and Sovereignty* (Duke University Press, 2006).

Nirmal Puwar teaches in the Sociology Department at Goldsmiths College of London. She is editor of *Feminist Review*, and author of *Space Invaders: Race, Gender and Bodies Out of Place* (Berg, 2004).

Jason Read teaches Philosophy at the University of Southern Maine. He is author of *The Micro-Politics of Capital: Marx and the Prehistory of the Present* (SUNY Press, 2003).

Judith Revel teaches at Université de Paris 1 Panthéon-Sorbonne. She contributes to «La bibliothèque foucaldienne, Michel Foucault au travail» (EHESS-ENS-CNRS) and she is editor of *Multitudes* and *Posse*. She wrote several articles and essays on the work of Michel Foucault and is author of *Foucault, le parole e i poteri. Dalla trasgressione letteraria alla resistenza politica* (Manifestolibri, 1996).

Andrew Ross is Chair of the Social and Cultural Analysis Department at New York University. He is co-founder of Faculty Democracy, the faculty organization that supported the graduate student strike at NYU in the 2005. He is the author of many books, including *No-Collar: The Humane Workplace and its Hidden Costs* (Basic Books, 2002) and *Fast Boat to China: Corporate Flight and the Consequences of Free Trade-Lessons from Shanghai* (Pantheon, 2006).

Ned Rossiter is Associate Professor of Network Cultures and the Univeristy of Nottingham Ningbo, China. A scholar and activist, he contributes to *Fibreculture* (www.fibreculture.org) and *Organized Networks* (orgnets.org). He is author of *Organized Networks: Media Theory, Creative Labour, New Institutions* (NAi Publishers, 2006).

Sunil Sahasrabudhey is member of the autonomous collective Vidya Ashram, Varanasi (India) that works on conflicts in the knowledge production. He is author of *The Peasant Movement Today* (South Asia Books, 1986).

Naoki Sakai teaches in the Asian Studies Department at Cornell University. He is co-founder of *Traces*. He is author of *Voices of the Past: The Status of Language in Eighteenth-Century Japanese Discorse* (Cornell University Press, 1992) and *Translation and Subjectivity: On "Japan" and Cultural Nationalism* (University of Minnesota Press, 2008).

Eileen Schell teaches at Syracuse University. She is an activist in the movement on the casualisation of academic labor in the US. She edited *Moving a Mountain: Transforming the Role of Contingent Faculty in Composition Studies and Higher Education* (National Council of Teachers, 2001).

Sanjay Sharma teaches in the School of Social Science at Brunel University, West London. He is editor of *Darkmatter*.

Jon Solomon teaches in the Graduate Institute of Future Studies at Tamkang University (Taiwan). He is a member of the *Traces* editorial board and edited with Naoki Sakai *Translation, Biopolitics, Colonial Difference* (Hong Kong University Press, 2006).

Universidad Experimental is a political collective that began in 2006 in Rosario (Argentina). They work on the project «cátedra experimental sobre producción de subjetividad» (universidadexperimental.wordpress.com).

Carlo Vercellone teaches at Université de Paris 1 Panthéon-Sorbonne. He is member of the program Matisse-ISYS (France) and the author of essays and articles on cognitive capitalism. He edited *Capitalismo cognitivo. Conoscenza e finanza nell'epoca postfordista* (Manifestolibri, 2006).

Vidya Ashram is an autonomous collective from Varanasi (India) that works on conflicts in the knowledge production (more info at www.vidyaashram. org/index.html).

Jeffrey Williams teaches in the Literary and Cultural Studies program at Carnegie Mellon University. He is involved in the campaign against student debt. He is author of *Critics at Work: Interviews 1992–2003* (New York University Press, 2004).

Xiang Biao is researcher at the Institute of Social and Cultural Anthropology at Oxford University. A scholar of labor and migration in Asia, he is the author of *Global "Body Shopping": An Indian International Labor System in the Information Technology Industry* (Princeton University Press, 2007).